CRYSTAL LAKE PUBLIC LIBRARY

3 2306 00379 5641

W9-BOB-546

OPPORTUN in

Aerospace Careers

331.702 MAP
Maples, Wallace R.,
Opportunities in aerospace
careers /

JAN — 2003

W 8/15
W3/18

W 71⊃⊂
W 8/09
W1/12

OPPORTUNITIES

in

PROPERTY OF C L P L

Aerospace Careers

REVISED EDITION

WALLACE R. MAPLES

VGM Career Books

Chicago   New York   San Francisco   Lisbon   London   Madrid   Mexico City
Milan   New Delhi   San Juan   Seoul   Singapore   Sydney   Toronto

The **McGraw·Hill** Companies

Library of Congress Cataloging-in-Publication Data

Maples, Wallace R., 1935–
    Opportunities in aerospace careers / Wallace Maples.—Rev. ed.
        p. cm.—(VGM opportunities series)
    Includes bibliographical references.
    ISBN 0-07-139050-2 (paperback)
    1. Aerospace engineering—Vocational guidance.   I. Title.
  II. Series.

  TL561 .M285   2002
  629.1'023—dc21   2002024981

Copyright © 2003 by The McGraw-Hill Companies, Inc. All rights reserved. Printed in the United States of America. Except as permitted under the United States Copyright Act of 1976, no part of this publication may be reproduced or distributed in any form or by any means, or stored in a database or retrieval system, without the prior written permission of the publisher.

1 2 3 4 5 6 7 8 9 0   LBM/LBM   1 0 9 8 7 6 5 4 3 2

ISBN 0-07-139050-2

McGraw-Hill books are available at special quantity discounts to use as premiums and sales promotions, or for use in corporate training programs. For more information, please write to the Director of Special Sales, Professional Publishing, McGraw-Hill, Two Penn Plaza, New York, NY 10121-2298. Or contact your local bookstore.

This book is printed on acid-free paper.

CONTENTS

   Education versus training. History of flight.

   Airline organizational structure. Airline pilot.
   Maintenance technician. Reservation sales agent.
   Flight attendant. Avionics technician. Other airline
   positions. Canadian airlines.

Foreword

As THIS BOOK goes to press, I am celebrating my fiftieth year as a pilot. Things were very different in the field of aviation half a century ago; among the differences was the lack of information on planning a career in aviation.

In 1945 a pilot earned private and commercial certificates and then perhaps obtained a flight instructor's rating (it was a rating then) and hoped to "build time" to go with an airline or into military flying. But times were bad then; there was a surplus of military and ex-military pilots in the year immediately following World War II, and such was also the case in the early 1990s.

Wallace Maples tells it like it is, without fake optimism. He lays out the requirements and expectations for the person who wants to make aerospace a career, and he suggests the best steps to take in reaching that goal.

All the important aerospace careers are covered in this book. Not every reader is interested in being a pilot. There are many other rewarding jobs in the field and, as the author indicates, there should be an increased demand in all areas for careerists.

This book would have been a great help to me in launching my career back in 1945. Dr. Maples has compiled the current information most needed for those aspiring to build a future in aviation.

William K. Kershner
Flight Instructor and Aviation Writer

Acknowledgments

It is impossible to compile such a gathering of facts, impressions, statistics, and information about broad career fields without the support of many people and numerous organizations. Not to recognize and thank them would be unconscionable.

The author is very much indebted to the following organizations for providing statistics on salaries, requirements for employment, and the numbers of people needed in the industry: Future Aviation Professionals of America (FAPA), National Business Aircraft Association (NBAA), Aero-Academe, National Aeronautics and Space Administration (NASA), American Airlines, Inc., the General Aviation Manufacturers Association, and the Federal Aviation Administration (FAA).

At the risk of omitting someone who has made a significant contribution, the following persons are recognized for donating time, effort, ideas, and moral support: Dr. Michael Schukert, Dr. Peggy Baty, Captain Stan Smartt, Dr. William Herrick, Commander Gary Odom, Captain Louis Smith (President of the Future Aviation Professionals of American), Alex Evans, Buck

Davis, Brett Fulford, A. Scott Crossfield, Lynn Crane, Irene Henley, William Kershner, and the aerospace faculty of Middle Tennessee State University.

To those who assisted and encouraged my entry into aerospace: Dr. Bealer Smotherman, Jack Sorenson, Dr. Merv Strickler, H. Miller Lanier, Dr. Ralph White, and Randall Wood.

Finally, with special thanks to my wife Carolyn; my three sons: Greg, Steve, and Bill; and my mother, Mary G. Maples, who "thought I could."

Acknowledgments for the Revised Edition

THE TEXT HAS been updated with the latest available research and statistics, without disturbing the narrative, which was written with the author's lifelong experience in the aviation industry. Dr. Maples, now retired, did not participate in the revision, but his thorough research guided the editor's task. Thanks to Aviation Now.com and its "Careers" editor, Carole Hedden; Air-Inc., the successor organization to Future Aviation Professionals of America; the FAA's Mr. Bill Shumann; and many others who gave their time and cooperation at a difficult time for the industry. The revision editor expresses his gratitude for their cooperation. The remaining errors are his fault alone.

Philip A. Perry
May 2002

1

THE BLUE FRONTIER: DEFINITION AND HISTORY OF AEROSPACE

AEROSPACE. YOU'VE HEARD the word, but what does it mean? The term combines *aero*, from aeronautics, referring to flight within the atmosphere, and *space*, signifying flight beyond the atmosphere. However, it really isn't quite so simple, because scientists have not agreed upon where that separation occurs. It is probably more proper to consider the space above us as gradually changing in terms of sustaining life without the aid of life-support equipment. Operations within that space above us provide the widest variety of career opportunities of almost any field of endeavor.

A full range of skill, training, and education is necessary to conceive, develop, build, pilot, and maintain the aircraft that fly above us. Aeronautical and astronautical engineers, machinists, managers, pilots, flight attendants, maintenance and avionics technicians, air traffic controllers, and astronauts are among the people employed in the hundreds of careers available in aerospace.

This guide will assist you in exploring the myriad of jobs available to you in aerospace. The chapters are devoted to exploring the types of jobs found within the variety of workplaces that make up this industry. You will learn about the levels of education required, the working conditions within the industry, the salaries earned by skilled workers and professionals, and the job outlook for the portion of the industry that excites you.

Education Versus Training

Several of the career fields in aerospace require the highest of educational levels, such as a doctorate in engineering, physics, or some other physical science. For such careers, you can anticipate a minimum of seven years of college, with two to three degrees earned on the road to success.

On the other hand, there are some aerospace careers for high school graduates that require no college, but rather some specialized training. Such careers may result in greater earnings than do some other careers that require three college degrees. The choice between education and training depends largely upon your career goals and to some degree will reflect a difference between what you may know and what you can do.

Education

Education focuses on what you know. It involves broad-based learning, which tends to urge the learner to sample many fields of knowledge, concentrating in the latter stages on one specific field, such as physics or engineering. Education prepares you more for the future in general—for developing, designing, and reordering what now exists and for coming up with new knowledge to create or improve the technology with which everyone must work.

Training

Training involves something you do. This may be a natural aptitude in mechanics, which allows you to work on jet engines or aircraft radios. Or it may involve a very different skill that helps you to control numerous airplanes within a finite airspace—sight unseen. Training prepares you for exceptional performance in a skilled position.

Making Your Own Choice

Education tends to teach a variety of knowledge, including alternative behaviors and ways of thinking, thus making people different in terms of how they apply that knowledge. Training tends to teach a common skill, making people more alike in what they do. The significance of this information for you involves what you want from a job or career. Do you wish to learn a skill quickly, which will allow you to earn a comfortable living until retirement, performing essentially the same tasks on a routine basis? Or do you wish to invest several years within formal education, learning the theoretical, abstract, and conceptual stages of a discipline? Education not only leads to essentially more creative work, but frequently leads to management positions in a career field. Although people may also rise to management levels from skilled positions and enjoy some freedom of expression, they are more likely to feel under pressure to perform beyond their educational preparation. Therefore, college education is recommended if you have managerial aspirations.

The aerospace industry, perhaps more so than any other industry, utilizes virtually every trade, skill, profession, and discipline of study known in modern times. Medical doctors, lawyers, analysts, engineers, accountants, finance specialists, and marketing personnel are but a few of the professionals who may work within aerospace. Skilled craft workers such as machinists, sheet metal workers, welders, carpenters, and pipe fitters may also be employed within aerospace. Nonskilled employees such as typists, drivers, receptionists, and building maintenance workers are needed within aerospace as well. Regardless of your education or training background, you may find a place among the numerous positions in aerospace.

In addition to the many general skills and professions utilized by aerospace firms, there are abundant aerospace-specific positions available. Aerospace must have pilots, aircraft maintenance technicians, air traffic controllers, flight dispatchers, reservationists, avionics technicians, and safety inspectors, to name a few. We'll learn about all of these positions as we explore the fascinating aerospace world in which we live.

History of Flight

The desire to fly has been a part of human nature throughout recorded history. Cave drawings, which are millions of years old, depict flight. Greek and Roman mythology tells a story of a father and son, Daedalus and Icarus, who supposedly escaped an island prison by building wings, gluing feathers on their bodies, and flying away. Chinese legends of some four thousand years ago allow us a glimpse into the desires of those who would fly. In fact, the

Chinese invented several items, such as kites (100 B.C.) and gunpowder (A.D. 900), that could have made flight possible.

We all know of Leonardo da Vinci's Renaissance drawings of the ornithopter, the parachute, and what we have come to know as the helicopter. Some believe he may have flown models of these flying machines.

The Montgolfier brothers of France were the first to launch live passengers into the "wild blue yonder," at least as far as recorded history indicates. They developed the hot air balloon, and in a demonstration for King Louis XVI and Marie Antoinette, sent aloft a rooster, a duck, and a sheep on September 19, 1783. Just two months later, they sent the first humans into the atmosphere. The world of flight had begun!

It would be some 120 years later before the Wright brothers of Dayton, Ohio, would launch the first powered, controlled flight of a heavier-than-air vehicle. Orville Wright flew for twelve seconds and traveled 120 feet on December 17, 1903, at Kitty Hawk, North Carolina. The entire length of that historic flight could take place inside some of today's cargo planes. It was very important, however, as it set the tone for future flight, in addition to proving that flight could take place. Wouldn't it be great to bring the Wright brothers back to see what they created? In fact, Orville Wright lived until 1948 and thus observed significant developments in aerospace, especially during World War II.

For thousands of years of recorded history, we did not fly. Then suddenly, within the span of one lifetime, we sent people to the moon at speeds in excess of twenty thousand miles per hour. What a tremendous leap in technology! And what a wonderful period of history for you to be alive in and to be able to contribute to the development of aerospace.

2

CAREERS WITH THE AIRLINES

PERHAPS NO INDUSTRY has changed so markedly as the U.S. airline industry has changed since 1990. During the early 1990s, U.S. airlines lost more money in four years—more than $10 billion—than they had earned cumulatively in their entire history. In addition to the billions of dollars lost by U.S. carriers, thousands of employees lost their jobs, many permanently. Two of the oldest and most respected carriers, Eastern Airlines and Pan American World Airways, closed their doors after a tremendous history of air service dating to the 1920s.

Regional carriers also met their demise in significant numbers, dropping from 250 in 1981 to 94 in 2001. Consolidation of air carriers continued through mergers and buyouts. Job prospects for pilots and maintenance technicians, which had been exceptional during the 1980s, now changed tremendously. These workers were being furloughed in record numbers. Some twenty-three hundred pilots were on furlough in 1995. But the year 2000 saw a record nineteen thousand pilots hired. Clearly it is an up and down marketplace. Although there will always be some positions available for newly trained airline workers, job applicants will have to become more competitive through education, training, licensing, and experience.

The largest U.S. airlines must use the broadest talent pool available in the entire aerospace industry. There is practically no skill, profession, or trade group that is not in some way useful to a large air carrier. The airlines hire pilots, maintenance technicians, lawyers, real estate specialists, managers of all descriptions, baggage handlers, engineers, and chefs. The list is nearly endless.

The U.S. airlines have been called by various names since their humble beginnings during the 1920s. They have been known as trunk carriers, major air carriers, airlines, intercity air transports, and domestic air carriers, to name a few. Today the airlines are divided into four categories on the basis of their annual gross earnings:

1. *Global carriers* earn in excess of $5 billion yearly, with at least $1 billion coming from international operations.
2. *Major carriers* earn in excess of $1 billion yearly.
3. *National carriers* earn between $100 million and $1 billion yearly.
4. *Regional carriers* earn less than $100 million yearly and employ at least fifty pilots.

Regional carriers are further divided into two categories according to their propulsion systems: they are considered either turboprop or turbojet carriers. It is with the regional carriers that many people find entry-level positions and work their way up within the organization, or move to larger carriers when they have enough experience.

Global and major carriers pay the highest wages and salaries and frequently offer better benefits. Although all airlines offer additional perquisites, or perks—that is, benefits given in addition to salary—the global and major carriers offer the greatest perks: free flights to their employees and to the immediate families of their employees. The number of flights an employee may obtain within a given year, and the family members who also qualify, will vary among the airlines. With some carriers, the length of one's employment will affect the perks. Carriers with international routes afford the employee travel to other nations as well. One can see that when an airline allows the wife or husband, all children, father and mother, and even brothers and sisters to fly virtually free, it adds to people's desire to work for the airlines.

Additional perks offered to employees are found in the form of discounted hotel rooms, cheaper car rentals, and visits to resort properties with which the carrier reciprocates. All of these factors must be considered when you review salary statistics. Several thousand dollars per year in cost savings accruing from perks can be added to the already excellent value of the base salary received. Even employees with smaller regional carriers that have code-sharing relationships with larger carriers are offered many of the same privileges. At the present time, these perks are relatively free from income tax. How long this will continue remains to be seen.

Airline Organizational Structure

To fully understand where you may work within an airline, it is necessary to look briefly at the organizational structure of the larger carriers. This will allow you to prepare yourself properly for the job you desire and to understand where you will be working within the structure.

The larger airlines generally are divided into at least four large working groups:

1. *Operations* covers the day-to-day functions of putting planes into the air, with job categories like pilot, flight attendant, and dispatcher.
2. *Maintenance* involves the daily and major checks on airplanes, including avionics, fueling, and overhaul, with job categories such as technician, avionics specialist, and ground crew.
3. *Marketing* may include positions such as sales, forecasting, advertising, reservations, and food services.
4. *Finance* includes purchasing, auditing, investment, borrowing capital funds, property acquisition, and aircraft purchases.

It is obvious that many functions performed within an airline are not listed in the brief summary above. You may obtain books from several sources that will offer a more in-depth look at the organization of airlines, so that you may become more familiar with the department in which you wish to work.

Management functions occur in all airline divisions within a line and staff framework, "line" referring to direct command and decision-making functions and "staff" having to do with support services. It is difficult to determine by title alone whether a particular manager is considered to be in a line function or a staff position.

That's enough about airline organization. You want to find out about the many specific jobs airlines offer. Let us first consider those that require very specialized training and education, plus certification by the Federal Aviation Administration (FAA).

Airline Pilot

Perhaps the most exotic, romantic, and exciting position to which one may aspire today is that of airline pilot. The word "pilot" conjures up glamorous images of being in charge, of making life-and-death decisions in a split second, and of exotic travel to faraway places. All of these attributes may be true at times. However, there is more truth to be found in a rather routine day of driving to the airport, looking over weather charts, going aboard the airplane, running through a checklist, starting engines, taxiing out for take-off, and flying without incident for several hours to another airport. Piloting is a way of earning a living—a rather good way for sure—but one with routine, consistent, and often boring work, not unlike jobs in other fields. It may surprise you to learn that many of the highest paid pilots work for airfreight companies like FedEx. Not as glamorous as flying passengers to Europe, maybe, but very well compensated.

The pilot flying for the larger airline has paid his or her dues before assuming command of a Boeing 747 with four hundred passengers aboard. It has taken the pilot years to work up to this level, often by flying in general aviation (encompassing business aviation, private aviation, and all nonmilitary and nonairline flights) or by serving in the military before being hired by a major airline.

Education

The pilot aspiring to the large carriers today will have a bachelor's degree from an accredited university. Although this was not the case for many current captains when they came into the airlines, it is unusual today for one to be hired without a college degree. Eighty percent of the pilots hired by global/major carriers these days hold a bachelor's degree. Nearly 15 percent also hold a master's degree. That leaves only 5 percent with fewer than four years of college. One needs to know that airlines have both soft and hard hiring requirements. Hard requirements refer to items for which there will be no deviation in hiring practices, such as FAA certification, health requirements, and criminal history. Soft requirements may involve education, correctable eyesight, and flight time. Soft requirements are more severe when there is a large pilot pool from which to choose. The mid-1980s saw airlines relax some requirements when pilots were in great demand.

If you aspire to rise to the level of pilot with the large airlines, be aware that your competition almost surely has a college degree. Several new hires will also have graduate degrees.

Certification

Pilots in training for future commercial flight positions will normally obtain a series of certificates beginning with the private pilot certificate and continuing through the instrument rating, the commercial certificate, the multiengine rating, and the air transport pilot (ATP) certificate, which is the "Ph.D." of pilot certificates. Even though the ATP is not required for initial hiring by some airlines, holding the certificate will enhance one's hiring potential.

Current FAA regulations allow a person to achieve the private pilot certificate in 35 flight hours, the commercial and instrument ratings in 190 hours, and the ATP in 1,500 hours. These are the minimum hours, and this assumes that the individual has had the proper instruction; passed written, oral, and flight examinations; and has the required hours of night, instrument, cross-country, and solo flight. One must also be of the required age according to FAA regulations. The average flight hours for those issued the private pilot certificate are in reality closer to 60 than 35 hours.

Airline pilots will continue to learn on the job, will go back for recurrent training, will keep up with the literature in their field, and will progress into larger aircraft until they reach their individual pinnacles of success.

About every ten to fifteen years, a new generation of passenger aircraft comes along and completely revolutionizes the industry. Aircraft such as the Boeing 767 and the Airbus 340, which came along in the 1980s, have now been joined by the Boeing 777 and the McDonnell Douglas MD-11. The latter two aircraft are larger, their engines have greater thrust, and they carry heavier payloads. These aircraft are capable of taxiing, taking off, flying a complex course with several changes of direction and altitude, landing, and taxiing off the runway without the pilot touching the controls. The pilot will program the onboard computers prior to leaving the gate, should an automated flight be desired. You can bet a new generation of aircraft is on the drawing boards now—Boeing's Sonic Cruiser concept is one idea of the future of passenger flight. The Airbus 380 series, carrying more than five hundred passengers, is set for commercial production by 2006.

Working Conditions

The airline pilot may not fly in excess of 100 hours per month or 1,000 hours per year, according to FAA regulations. Many people confuse that with the total workload of a pilot. Nothing could be further from the truth. The pilot spends countless hours in the dispatch office planning trips, hours commuting to work from as far away as several hundred miles, working on reports, briefing crews, attending flight recurrent training or management schools, and performing other duties as designated by the company. Many pilots represent their companies in public speaking engagements, on committees for pilot welfare, and on national committees that work toward the enhancement of flight safety. Add to this the major layovers required of international and long-route domestic flights, and you can see that the pilot is quite busy over long periods of time. The pilot flies on average 75 hours per month and works an additional 120 hours on the ground.

Of course, the major part of the profession involves what every pilot loves the most: flying. The pilot spent thousands of dollars and countless hours of preparation getting to the cockpit and thereby deserves all of the rewards and respect that accrue to the position.

Members of ethnic minorities and women were excluded from the cockpits of the major carriers for years, despite the contributions they made to popularize flight. Such is not the case today. Although less than 1 percent of current airline pilots are African-American, this figure is likely to increase in the coming decades as more African-Americans enter flight training programs. American Airlines in 1964 voluntarily hired the first African-American pilot to be employed by a major carrier.

Female pilots have been hired by the airlines in increasing numbers only since 1973, when the regional carrier Frontier Airlines hired Emily Warner. It was a tough struggle for her and one she was not sure she would ever win. When she was hired, she had a total of seven thousand hours of flying time. The first woman hired by a major carrier was Bonnie Tiburzi, who was hired by American Airlines in 1973. Approximately 2 percent of the pilots with global and major airlines are women. United Airlines has the best hiring record, with Delta Air Lines having the worst.

The struggle by women to occupy equal status with men in the cockpit traces from 1911, when Harriet Quimby became the first American woman to earn a pilot certificate. Some interesting books about the trials and tribulations of female pilots are included in Appendix B.

Salary

Earnings for airline pilots who fly with the global carriers are among the highest salaried jobs in America. It has been said that the average earnings of these pilots are greater than the average salaries of medical doctors. If not, such earnings must surely approach those of medical professionals.

A pilot with a global carrier, with ten years of service, earns an average of $143,000, plus benefits, and a per diem—living expenses when away from the crew base. This is an average; salaries vary considerably among even the global carriers. Major carrier pilots with ten years of service easily earn $100,000-plus annually; in fact, in a 2001 survey by AIR-Inc., monthly pay averaged $12,400 for tenth-year pilots at major U.S. carriers such as American, Northwest, and United. Remember that the starting pilot salary for global and major carriers hovers around $30,000 to $35,000 per year for first or second officers at entry level.

Salaries for pilots with national air carriers and the various levels of regional carriers will vary much more than with the global and major carriers. Regional pilots on turbojets will average around

$79,000, according to National Business Aviation Association (NBAA) reports, with turboprop pilots averaging $79,000 as well. Starting salaries for Air Line Pilots Association (ALPA) union pilots at entry level (first officer) with regional carriers were $23,000. Although the turnover rate within regional airlines was quite high during the mid-1980s, that has slowed considerably, with many pilots now making a career with the regional carriers.

Many factors must be considered when comparing careers, especially where salary is concerned. Longevity with a single airline is crucial to pay levels, but other items are also important. The type of aircraft flown, whether routes flown are domestic or international, whether the airline is unionized, and if there is pay for time away from home can make a considerable difference in the annual salary. Thus, the salary of an airline captain whom you may know could be tens of thousands of dollars on either side of the average. Some pilots for small airlines fly for salaries below the poverty level.

One way to understand the wide variation of salaries is to look at the range as well as the average. The range takes into consideration the high and the low for a given position. Industry figures show that the range for global air carrier captains, making the maximum base salary, varies from a low of $108,000 up to $200,000. Another factor to consider is whether a salary is earned or quoted only on the base-pay scale. Earned salaries tend to be higher. It is generally known that many captains earn more than $200,000 per year, although their base salaries are considerably lower. Depending upon the source consulted, the thirty-year career of a major airline pilot can gross between $4 million and $7 million dollars for the lucky person.

Employment Outlook

So you ask, "OK, great salary, great working conditions, but what are my chances of finding employment as a pilot?" The FAA projects a total airline pilot hiring need of 100,264 by 2004. Your chances are better now than in the recent past. No one needs to know that the FAA is usually quite optimistic. However, if one combines the known pilot requirements, the number of additional nonreplacement aircraft purchased and optioned, and the increased traffic that will definitely occur, the FAA figure may be no more than 10,000 or so on the optimistic side for the major airlines. Nearly 7,000 pilots were hired by all U.S. carriers in 1994. This was the biggest hiring year since the mid-1980s. Then in 2000, more than 19,000 pilots were hired by all airlines, of which about 10,000 went to the major carriers and the national airlines. Hiring was expected to level off to 14,500 for 2002. Given the expected number of retirements and the air traffic growth projected through 2020, in this market your hiring chances are rather good, everything else being equal.

Increasingly, American pilots are finding jobs with international carriers or carriers in other countries. Although such positions are equally difficult to locate, at least twenty-six foreign carriers list American pilots and some seven leasing firms contract with American pilots. Your chances are enhanced if you speak one or more foreign languages and hold international flight certificates. The greater your flight experience, the more likely you will find an international position.

Another opportunity exists with start-up airlines for pilots willing to risk their funds. New airlines wishing to fill a niche recruit qualified pilots, buy used aircraft, and establish operations from an air carrier airport. These "upstart" airlines may require pilots to buy into the company in amounts that can reach up to $50,000. One must be very careful with such airlines. It may never be approved or may not raise sufficient monies to stay in business. However, if you make a wise selection, get in on the ground floor, and the airline succeeds, you reap the rewards of a highly speculative economic endeavor. For the few, riches abound.

The Bottom Line

Flying for the scheduled airlines can provide an excellent lifestyle. In fact, a major airline executive commented that being a pilot is not a career at all; it is a way of life. The pay is great, the travel can be extensive, and the working conditions are generally excellent. The employment opportunities, though having been among the worst ever during the early 1990s, are improving as more airlines hire new pilots. In 2001 most U.S. airlines operated at a loss. Long-term prospects look good, however, as global air passenger and cargo traffic may double by 2020. By then, Boeing predicts, the world fleet of big jets will number almost thirty-three thousand.

The major disadvantages of becoming an airline pilot are the cost of the various certificates, ranging from $15,000 to $25,000; the amount of dues-paying, or seasoning time, required to qualify for airline employment; and the fact that air carrier pilots must retire at age sixty. And despite the fact that pilots may obtain free flights for family members, the nature of their job nevertheless requires a fair amount of time away from home and family. This is especially true in the earlier years of one's career when flying reserve, and then again late in a career, when one assumes command of lengthy international training flights.

Maintenance Technician

Perhaps the greatest need in the aerospace field today is for maintenance personnel. Need has to do with the lack of qualified workers in skilled areas for which an extended amount of time or formal schooling is required. The aviation maintenance technician (AMT) is the backbone of the airline. Without this technician, the airplane does not fly, and the remaining airline employees are out of work. Safety is foremost in the mind of everyone who works for an airline. Robert Crandall, president of American Airlines, has indicated that he feels personally responsible for safety within American Airlines. When the head of any corporation takes responsibility for any attribute or characteristic of that company, one can be assured that it is on the mind of everyone else within the company.

The technician in today's aerospace environment is confronting a very different setting than that experienced by his or her predecessors. The technology has changed by quantum leaps within a very short period. Much of the change came about with the introduction of the jet airplane in commercial service. The first U.S. airline to fly a pure jet was National Airlines in 1958. Yet it took several years to replace the piston engine, even in the airlines. Today we not only have the jet, but we also have increasingly more complicated engines, much larger engines, and the new glass cockpit. All of the analog instrument technology is being replaced by a cathode ray tube (CRT), a small, computer-type screen—the "glass cockpit." The engine instruments in which the pilot once placed so much faith now may not appear unless the pilot calls them up or the computer that monitors the engines wishes to alert the pilot to a problem. Maintenance technicians not only confront new instrumentation and engines, but also composite materials being utilized in place of all-metal structures. Anticipated changes are expected to be even greater in the foreseeable future.

Education

The aviation maintenance technician—or mechanic, as he or she may be referred to in some areas—comes to that trade by several routes. The three main ways to become a technician are:

1. by experience, working under the guidance of a certified technician
2. by formal training in a school certified by the FAA
3. by experience and training while serving in the military, with subsequent certification by the FAA

Whichever you choose, the target to shoot for is FAA certification as an airframe and power plant technician. If you come to such certification via experience, you must spend a minimum of eighteen months of full-time work in each specialty under the direction of one or more certified technicians. You may choose to attend a formal school. This may be a vocational school, one associated with a high school, an associate degree program, or a maintenance management program, wherein one can earn both the bachelor's degree and the requisite certificates. The school must be an FAA-certified maintenance technician school. Another method of obtaining education is through a technical school operated by a branch of the military and by working in that area during military service. The FAA has recently made it easier for AMTs with military experience to obtain civilian certification.

Certification

The maintenance technician must have either an airframe certificate or a power plant certificate, or both. The only exception to this is to work in a certified repair station in a given specialty, such as welding, metal forming, or engine repair. The technician may obtain a repair certificate after at least eighteen months of practical experience in the duties of the specific job for which he or she is employed.

The airframe and power plant certificate, also called the A&P, is awarded by the FAA when the successful applicant has been recommended by either the school, the repair station, or the technician under which the person has apprenticed, or he or she presents military documentation of schooling, plus practical experience. The applicant must, in addition to experience and schooling, take written, oral, and practical examinations given by the FAA or by a designated examiner. There are no shortcuts to success.

After a maintenance technician with an A&P works for some time in the field, he or she probably will wish to achieve the next level of certification. This is called the inspector authorization (IA) and may be given to the A&P technician upon application to the local FAA office. The technician must be an experienced person, must be capable of effective supervision of colleagues, and must have the availability of an up-to-date technical library of airworthiness directives and other FAA data.

Working Conditions

The maintenance technician works in a variety of places, even within an airline. If you like to work under pressure, with rarely a dull moment, working on the line at the many airports served by your airline is the place to be. The technician will often make rapid repairs, change tires, replace instruments, or make decisions about grounding the plane—that is, not allowing it to continue to fly without repairs that may be too extensive to maintain that airplane's schedule.

The technician has the best of technology to assist him or her in making decisions about a particular airplane. If the pilot calls ahead that she or he is encountering a problem, the technician goes directly to the computer, which is usually in contact with the airline's maintenance base. The technician calls up the record of the specific airplane, which lists everything done on that individual plane since it was purchased. The technician usually will call up only the information for the most recent week or the past couple of days. This information helps the technician determine what the problem might be. He or she may also consult maintenance manuals on this specific type of airplane and discuss the problem with other technicians. The computer will not only assist in making a decision, but will also show whether the necessary parts are available at the airport. If not, the technician can have the parts delivered.

When the airplane arrives, the technician further analyzes the problem and makes a decision as to what is needed. One of the disadvantages of working as a technician at the airport is weather. The airplane may be too large to push into a hangar, so the technician often works outside. The job may be in Chicago in January, with winds of forty miles per hour and subzero temperatures that cut to the bone. Or it may be in El Paso in July, with even stronger winds and temperatures hovering around one hundred degrees Fahrenheit. Of course, it might be in New Orleans in April and be just perfect.

There are basically six types of maintenance checks that are accomplished on an airplane. Normally only two of these are completed without a hangar and specialized equipment. If you are working at a maintenance or overhaul base, you will be working with hundreds of other technicians and likely will be doing shift work, as these bases work around the clock. One of the major carriers, which already has a huge maintenance base, has recently added another at a cost of some $400 million. The new facility will employ twenty-five hundred technicians immediately and will grow to forty-five hundred technicians. No small operation, this maintenance business.

Aside from airlines, the maintenance technician will find employment with the major airframe and engine manufacturers, the military, and within general aviation. These areas of employment are covered in other chapters of this book.

Salary

The salary levels of the maintenance technician vary with experience, certification, level of responsibility, and geographic region of the nation, as well as with the type of company for which the technician works. Among the airlines, the major carriers pay the highest average salary. In a 2001 survey, a national airline was paying the highest maximum average for a technician, $28 per hour. Global and major airlines probably pay even more. Tables 2.1 and 2.2 give some examples of hourly salary ranges for maintenance technicians at national and regional airlines.

Table 2.1 Maintenance Technician Salaries

Type of U.S. Carrier	Base Rate	Top
Major Airline	$19.43	$28.00
Regional (East Coast)	$11.69	$18.57
Regional (Pacific Northwest)	$14.93	$23.41
Regional (North Central)	$11.48	$20.80

Source: AMFA (Aircraft Mechanics Fraternal Association), 2002.

Employment Outlook

Forecasts by the FAA, the Future Aviation Professionals of America (FAPA), and the Federal Bureau of Labor indicate a bright future for the AMT. Scheduled airlines employ some 68,000 technicians. Although the global/major airlines had more than 3,500 AMTs on furlough in 1995, all scheduled carriers combined furloughed only 3,700 technicians. U.S. carriers had hired some 3,500 AMTs in 1994.

Annual attrition is expected to be 5 percent at global/major carriers, 10 percent at regional airlines, 7 percent for government

Table 2.2 Airline Starting Pay

Airline	Starting Hourly Pay
Delta	$15.27
Southwest	$16.70
US Airways	$16.65
Continental	$13.11
American	$14.18
United	$15.17
UPS	$13.40
FedEx	$16.71
American Trans Air	$10.71

Source: AviationNow.com/McGraw-Hill; Aircraft Mechanics Fraternal Association, 2001.

employed AMTs, and 10 percent for general aviation operations. Beyond 2004, the FAA predicts annual hiring of AMTs to reach 14,000. In 2001 there were between 135,000 and 140,000 trained mechanics, with room in the job market for many more. The FAA also predicts an actual shortage of fully qualified technicians. One must understand that "fully qualified" means to have training and experience on "heavy iron," composite structures, and new nondestructive testing techniques. AMTs not so qualified will be stuck at the low end of the hiring spectrum.

Overseas job prospects for AMTs are even better than for pilots, with some salaries at very high levels. The People's Republic of China is building airports, buying airplanes, and expanding operations by quantum leaps. The Mideast holds excellent prospects, as do other areas of the Pacific Rim nations. Excellent tax advantages exist for those willing to remain out of the United States for 270 days each year. Up to $70,000 may be exempt, depending upon one's particular tax circumstances.

The Bottom Line

The long-term job outlook for AMTs looks favorable through 2010. Most vacancies that occur will be for "fully qualified" technicians, which means having had schooling and experience with composite materials, glass-cockpit avionics, large turbine engines, and nondestructive testing. Not everyone will start an AMT career with such experience. You will have to earn your way up in the system by making progressive moves to more complex aircraft as you learn. If you are good with your hands, like mechanical challenges, and are adept at reading and interpreting what you read, a maintenance technician career could be the perfect choice for you.

Reservation Sales Agent

Airline reservations may be made with a travel agency or directly with the airline. Although many reservations are made through a travel agency, all airlines of any size will have a reservations system, or they will contract with a larger airline to handle reservations on their behalf.

Reservations made directly with the airline may be accomplished by phone or by walking into one of a variety of ticket offices operated by the airline. We are probably most familiar with reservations made by phone or by going online to an airline's or discount ticket-seller's website. Airlines, depending upon their size and desired visibility, may have a downtown city ticket office (CTO) or may share a ticket office with other airlines in large hotels or in business districts. They may also have a ticket office located at large military bases, referred to as a joint airline military ticket office (JAMTO), usually staffed by agents from several carriers. Wherever the traveler purchases the airline ticket, contact for the reservation itself was either made online or by phone. Thus, we need to consider the reservation sales agent in our discussion of various airline careers. The airlines employ about fifty-four thousand agents.

Education

The reservation sales agent is not required to have any specific level of education beyond high school. However, the airline desires as highly educated a person as possible. Although the customer does not see the agent, the agent may be the first contact between the airline and a customer, who is referred to as a client in the industry. The agent "becomes" the airline to the client. Speed, efficiency, courtesy, and providing what the client wants are all sales techniques that the experienced agent provides. Even though education cannot guarantee skill in these techniques, it usually can enhance the probability of the agent providing a better service. Airline reservation sales agents work not only with clients, but also, in some instances, with travel agents who call on behalf of their clients. Travel agents can be more demanding, so patience and competence become key virtues for the airline reservationist.

What are some of the attributes of an agent that are desired by the airline? A pleasing telephone voice and friendly personality that comes across through voice alone are chief attributes. The airline prefers someone with a knowledge of geography, which will enhance the agent's ability to make key connections for clients traveling to hard-to-reach destinations. An agent should have sharp mathematics skills, keen reasoning ability, and good judgment. The airline also would like someone who has experience with a computer or keyboard, as the agent will use the computer throughout the workday. Airline computers differ from the systems used in the general business world, so an agent must be trained to use the specific airline system. Travel schools usually offer some computer training, and the airlines themselves train reservation agents prior to their first contact with clients or travel agents. Top airline computer systems include American's SABRE, United's APOLLO, and Continental's System One. The Internet has changed the nature of the ticket reservations business, as more business is done through electronic commerce.

Working Conditions

The airline reservation sales agent usually works in a large central office answering customer questions by phone and booking customer reservations. The working conditions are typically pleasant, clean, and climate-controlled. The majority of agents enjoy each other's company as they encounter similar problems and amusing circumstances.

The problems associated with the agent's work are irregular hours, pressure of handling calls expeditiously, and trying to pacify the traveler under stressful conditions. Eyestrain and wrist problems from hours on the computer are occupational hazards.

Salary

Industry-wide information on the salaries of reservation sales agents is not available. One estimate sets the hourly wage at $11.66. That's the per hour median wage calculated by the Bureau of Labor Statistics for reservation sales personnel for 2001. It works out to a little more than $23,000 a year. Industry salary averages ranged from $12,000 to $38,000 a year in 1995. One major carrier paid new workers somewhat less, on the basis of an A and B pay scale, the levels of which reach parity in the sixth year of employment. A-scale salaries go to agents who have already worked for the company, while B-scale wages are paid to new hires in an effort to reduce labor costs. The B-scale agent receives $14,112 annually to start. Both agents make $28,752 during their sixth year, when they reach parity. The pay scale for the tenth year is $35,316. Supervisors with ten years would average $41,672. Other positions, largely administrative or managerial, associated with this type of work are sales manager and regional director. Salaries are commensurate with the level of responsibility.

Employment Outlook

The need for reservation agents is rather constant. The employment of such agents depends upon turnover from such factors as retirement, burnout, termination, and the normal fluctuations of the industry during economic changes. To apply for a job, contact the airline for which you wish to work. A list of major airline corporate addresses appears in Appendix A. It is, of course, helpful if you live in or near the city where the reservations center is located. You may determine that by calling the airline for which you wish to be an agent.

The Bottom Line

Reservation agents can make an excellent income after a few years of work with a company. Although the work is fast-paced and sometimes stressful, successful agents learn to enjoy it. Full-time agents enjoy all the perks of airline employees, such as free or greatly discounted flight tickets, pensions, benefits, stock options, and insurance. Some airlines also employ part-time agents. Though such employees typically do not qualify for the perks, they are able to be a part of the industry while having more time for other activities outside of work. If you have the kind of special personality that communicates effectively by voice alone, you may do well in the world of the reservation agent.

Flight Attendant

The flight attendant is the person who may be most responsible for the client's overall impression of the airline. The client never actually sees the reservation agent, who works by phone from a remote location. The client is in contact with the person who issues the boarding pass for only a few moments. The gate attendant is usually too busy to be involved with each client for very long. And the pilots almost never come in direct contact with the client, except to say goodbye when the passenger deplanes. As the airline's most visible representative, the flight attendant is left to mold the company image.

The flight attendant was formerly referred to as a stewardess, as the career field until recently was totally dominated by women. This came about because the first flight attendants were nurses, members of another profession heavily populated by women. The attendants were aboard primarily to care for the apprehensive air traveler during these early days. Early commercial flights were noisy, rarely climate-controlled, and not pressurized, which could cause nausea. Airplanes at that time were frequently caught in rough air, since they could not climb high enough to get above the weather. A flight attendant/nurse could be very valuable.

Today flight conditions are smoother, and the nurse is no longer a necessity. However, a new breed of flight attendant has evolved. The passenger has come to expect more service during the flight. The flights are shorter in duration, the number of passengers per flight is increasing, and competition among the airlines is stiffer. This certainly requires a flight attendant who not only knows what to do and can do it quickly, but who also has a friendly personality and relates well to others.

Education

The major airlines wish to hire college graduates if at all possible. Practically all of the major carriers indicate in their employment literature that they prefer at least two years of college or two years of equivalent business experience. Some will accept other work experiences that involve considerable public contact in lieu of some college. The number of flight attendants with a college degree is increasing. This is not unique, as we see that many of the career fields that once hired high school graduates now require a college degree for entry.

You can obtain a feel for the type of courses to take by reviewing a specific airline's requirements for a flight attendant. You may receive the requirements by writing or calling a particular airline of your choice. You will see such requirements as good English usage, effective conversational skills, and foreign language being desirable. The airline also looks for attributes that may not be learned in a classroom setting, such as maturity, emotional stability, an outgoing personality, poise, ability to work under stress, and flexibility in terms of relocating.

The training of a flight attendant usually requires from three to seven weeks, with larger airlines imposing greater requirements. The majority of training is conducted by the hiring airline. The airline may pay the future attendant a modest salary and provide lodging and meals during the training, as well as free transportation to the training site. Not everyone accepted for training will graduate from the program. Several people will remove themselves from training after discovering that the job was not what they thought. Others will be dropped from training by the airline because they do not meet the requirements of the training program. One major airline indicated that more trainees leave voluntarily than the airline drops.

The training is developed around three major areas of concern: flight safety, customer service, and marketing. The passenger is rarely aware of the tremendous amount of safety training required of the flight attendant. The FAA lists very specific functions that each attendant must be able to perform, along with certain regulations that each attendant must know. The FAA also requires recurrent training each year on safety factors related to the type of aircraft to which the attendant is assigned. Most airlines exceed the FAA requirements in training attendants on safety measures. Attendants will be aware of emergency exits, methods of getting out of the aircraft, and how to be ready for unique events like ditching over water. The rigorous training may include simulation of emergency situations, such as trying to find exits and remove passengers in a plane filled with dense smoke. Flight attendants also will be proficient in cardiopulmonary resuscitation (CPR) and in emergency measures for heart attacks, extracting food lodged in someone's throat, and a dozen other emergency procedures.

The airline and the FAA hope that no attendant will ever have to utilize emergency procedures, but reality suggests that many will. There are numerous and recent accounts of heroic measures taken by attendants both on board and during a crash. Attendants have delivered babies, maintained CPR on heart attack victims, calmed hijackers and terrorists who had taken over a plane, moved through the aircraft ministering to numerous passengers when half the plane's roof had ripped off, and performed other unusual activities for which their training prepared them. Some were capable of rising to the unexpected for which no training can prepare.

Another element of training, and the one more frequently encountered on the job, is the everyday duty of welcoming passengers aboard, serving them food and drink, and wishing them a good flight. This element takes up a considerable period of training time, for it is the routine in which the attendant will spend the majority of the working flight. It also involves the third element of training—marketing—that sells company services and is becoming an increasingly important part of the flight attendant's job description.

Working Conditions

Some of the job functions of the flight attendant were covered in the section on training. When a new flight originates at a particular airport, the flight attendant crew will have arrived several minutes prior to the scheduled flight. The attendants will meet with the captain, who will brief them on the flight. Such items as weather, passenger load, expected delays, and any other unique features of the flight are discussed. Sometimes only the senior attendant meets with the captain and will then pass information on to the other attendants. The attendants will then go aboard the airplane and check on conditions such as food and drink supplies, whether the cleaning crew was thorough, if everything is in place as it should be, and whether the proper forms and safety equipment are aboard.

One or more of the attendants will stand at the gate to take tickets or look at the boarding passes of oncoming passengers. Another attendant will be just inside the cabin door greeting passengers and assisting those who need extra help. Particular attention is paid to small children, children traveling without parents, handicapped persons, and clients who are flying first class. The major chore is to get everyone seated, make sure their carry-on items are properly stowed, and see that conditions conform to FAA requirements.

As the aircraft begins to taxi, one attendant will read or recite the safety information required by the FAA. Such information relates to smoking restrictions, placing seat backs and tray tables in the upright position, having safety belts fastened, and making sure carry-on items are placed under the seat or in the closed overhead bins. As this attendant is talking, the other attendants are stationed throughout the airplane, demonstrating the safety measures to the passengers. On large aircraft, the entire orientation may be shown on screens. When the announcement is completed, all attendants will move throughout the cabin to confirm that their directions were followed. The captain will announce to the attendants to be seated for takeoff or will sound a gong that will alert the attendants.

As soon as the airplane has reached cruising altitude, the attendants will begin to see to passenger needs. They may serve a snack or a full meal, hand out reading material, or provide pillows and blankets if the trip is an extended one. Headsets are quite popular for extended flights, where a movie may be screened. Some flights have video games that may be rented and telephones with which passengers may call people on the ground. The future is already here aboard several aircraft, which are equipped with video screens in the seat backs. Up to four channels may be selected on these sets. First-class passengers may be served a seven-course meal on international flights, including champagne and many different wines. The attendant must be well versed in the niceties of life to compete in today's market.

Upon arrival at the designated airport, the attendants will again ensure that safety precautions are on the minds of all passengers. After the passengers have deplaned, the attendants may straighten up for the next group or may fill out numerous forms required by the airline and the FAA. Or they may, like some passengers, hurry to catch the next flight. It is not uncommon for both flight crew and flight attendants to change planes in the hub airports, just as passengers do.

Attendants typically work sixty-five to eighty-five flying hours per month. They may have up to eighty hours of nonflight duty time per month as well. Some of this may involve additional training, layover time, and paperwork. Supervisors will have additional duties. FAA regulations and the contract that is negotiated between the flight attendants' union and airline management determine flight time and duty hours. The majority of attendants are union members. Contracts are normally negotiated for a period of three years. Some unionized attendants have had to go on strike to obtain the benefits they desire. However, in recent years most union strikes have met with disaster.

Flight assignment is usually based on seniority. The attendants "bid their flights," that is they list their preferences, in the same manner as do the pilots. Normally the longer the attendant has been with the airline, the better the opportunity for being assigned to desired flights. New attendants may have to wait several years before being assigned to the more sought-after international flights. There are some exceptions to this. The need for attendants who are fluent in languages other than English may allow a new graduate who speaks a second language to be assigned to international flights. Such flights pay more and afford a greater number of days off than do domestic flights. The normal domestic flight scenario is two days flying and three days off. The international flight is two flying and five off. An attendant can make as few as three international flights per month for a full month's pay.

Flight attendants who have seniority can allow their flights, which are usually the more desirable flights, to pass to someone else and simply take time off. This gives flexibility to the lifestyle of the attendant. She or he may wish to do something else for a while, like travel, write, go to school, or stay at home with a new baby. Whatever the reason, it can be arranged. Some airlines will release an attendant for up to a year to complete college and may offer additional financial incentives to do so. Some airlines allow attendants to be part-time employees, working perhaps only one or two flights per month.

Salary

Flight attendants receive a rather good salary for the time they put into their work. However, one should understand that no salary adequately compensates a person who may face the danger that can confront the attendant in case of disaster in the air. Flying is generally safe. No other form of transportation approaches the safety record of the airlines. But at thirty thousand feet, traveling at five hundred miles per hour, anything can happen.

The airlines vary in what they pay attendants. Competing airlines tend to pay similar wages. National airlines have a competitive wage structure, and other levels of carrier will be similar. One recent development in the salary of attendants is referred to as A-scale and B-scale, which is somewhat similar to that described above for reservation sales agents. New attendants are hired at a lower salary than the more senior attendants are. They may reach parity at some point. Some believe that such a pay scale makes for a strained working climate.

According to the Future Aviation Professionals of America (FAPA), which offered a flight attendant employment referral service, the average beginning base salary for an attendant with a global airline was $14,796 per year during the 1990s. The fifth-year attendant averages $20,076 maximum, and the senior attendant up to $31,692. Obviously, some airlines pay above the average, some below. In 2002 one of the biggest U.S.-based carriers paid $15,500 to new hires for full-time work on domestic flights (defined as sixty-five hours a month), plus $19 an hour for extra hours up to eighty-five hours a month. A tenth-year attendant received $30,672 a year plus $39 an hour for extra hours. No one can work more than ninety hours a month, under this union contract. Duty on international flights pays a higher base rate.

Another factor that must be considered is that attendants are paid a per-hour rate for expenses when on duty. In a recent year, an attendant could earn an additional $600 per month—tax free—which came to $7,260 per year. The amount varies, based on cost of living.

Employment Outlook

In 2001 there were about 126,000 flight attendants working in the United States. The low end of their salary range was $18,000 and the median was $38,800, the Bureau of Labor Statistics estimates. Beginning flight attendants earned a median salary of just over $14,800 in 2001, reported the Association of Flight Attendants, a national union. The employment outlook for flight attendants is improving from where it was during the first half of the 1990s. In fact, except in really poor economic times, when everyone is affected, flight attendants have good prospects for employment. There has been an increase in routes and the number of aircraft operated by airlines since deregulation of the industry in 1978. There isn't a considerable turnover of attendants, although burnout claims some. Early retirement certainly affects the industry, as older attendants tend to desire more stability of family and geography.

One change that has come about in recent years, however, is that many flight attendants are flying for longer. Years ago, a stewardess could be fired if she gained weight, got married, or simply became "too old," the standards being arbitrarily decided by the employer. The airlines wanted young, single, attractive women as a lure for male business travelers. Today, because of antidiscrimination legislation, a flight attendant may be female or male, single or married, with or without children, and of any race or ethnic origin. Height and weight restrictions have been eased, and the attendant may fly as long as she or he is physically fit, or until age seventy. Some carriers are even hiring flight attendants who are presently fifty years of age and older.

The major and global airlines employ over 74 percent of all attendants with U.S. carriers. The national airlines employ 6 percent of the attendant workforce. The major domiciles and the larger bases will be where the greatest number of attendants will be based. Some airlines allow their attendants to commute—that is, to live at a distant place and catch nonworking flights to their assigned base. Most airlines do not allow reserve attendants to commute. You may have to move to the assigned base city until you have enough seniority to get off reserve. Some bases are "very senior," and you could be on reserve for years.

The Bottom Line

Being a flight attendant can be exciting. It can allow you to meet new people, sometimes very important people. You certainly get to travel. You also have excellent travel benefits during your free time, which will allow you to see the world at very little expense. With several airlines, your family receives some free travel and additional discounted travel. The pay is good for the time worked. There are other liberal benefits such as stock options, bonuses when the airline is doing well financially, insurance programs, and retirement. Disadvantages of a career as a flight attendant include erratic schedules that may conflict with family activities; physical wear and tear, especially on the feet; problems with unpleasant passengers; and the slim possibility of an accident aboard the plane. But most flight attendants believe that the enormous benefits far outweigh these drawbacks. Being a flight attendant is something you could really get up in the air about!

Avionics Technician

There was a time in the aviation industry when the avionics technician was basically an airframe or power plant technician with some additional knowledge or experience with radios. Radios were used primarily for communication. That era has long since passed. The avionics technician is a specialist in aviation electronics and may even further specialize in particular systems of communication and navigation.

The crowded sky is kept safe, to a large degree, by the electronic devices installed in the airplanes, which allow communication through similar devices on the ground. The air traffic controller of a bygone era maintained aircraft separation principally by talking with the pilots and interpreting information given by those pilots. Today the radar screen contains a blip representing the airplane, and also its flight number, the altitude at which it is flying, its direction, and its speed. Some airplanes have equipment on board that will monitor other aircraft in the vicinity. It will even alert the pilot of an impending collision and suggest what action to take. The FAA is also funding the development of new digital technology for NEXCOM ground/air communication, a next-generation system incorporating VDL-3 avionics that will replace ground radio communication between the pilot and the air traffic controller. One can readily see the extent to which the avionics technician of the future must be trained.

Education

The avionics technician may receive formal education in a variety of ways. The airline industry would prefer that the technician possess the airframe and power plant (A&P) certification, along with the appropriate Federal Communications Commission (FCC) license. There is reason to believe that the impending shortage of avionics technicians will cause a major separation of avionics from the A&P, such that the majority of technicians will not likely have education in both. The educational process is becoming too complex and protracted to appropriately educate for such a broadly experienced person.

Avionics technicians are educated at all levels and in all types of schools, just like A&P technicians. Colleges, universities, junior colleges, technical schools, a few high schools, and a large representation of proprietary (profit-making) schools educate the majority of avionics personnel. The military also contributes to such training. A typical program of training will last from fourteen to twenty-four months. The majority will be between eighteen and twenty-four months in length.

Basic electronics is essential to a thorough understanding of avionics. The potential technician should like aviation, be competent in mathematics, and be capable of communicating effectively. There is a greater possibility of a person doing well in avionics if the person understands the aviation environment. It is one thing to understand a principle that works on a test bench, but it is altogether different in real life to realize the stress of going from sea level to forty thousand feet several times per day, as airplanes do.

Certification

The certification of avionics technicians is different from that of A&P technicians. One difference is that the avionics technician's license comes not from the FAA, but from the FCC. There are several levels of licensing related to the different types of equipment serviced and what the technician is allowed to do to the equipment. For example, the avionics technician does not install or remove avionics equipment from the aircraft unless the technician also has an A&P certificate. What the avionics technician does to the equipment depends upon the level of FCC license held.

Working Conditions

The environment in which the avionics technician works is friendlier, at least in terms of the weather, than that of the A&P. Most avionics work is accomplished indoors "on the bench"—that is, inside an avionics laboratory. Some outside work may be required in the nose cone of the aircraft, which contains the radar equipment. Avionics equipment is normally quite clean and free of oil and grease, thus the avionics technician has a more hygienic environment in which to work. The equipment is normally enclosed and in modules that are easy to handle.

Salary

Avionics technicians earned a median $19.86 an hour in 2000. Salaries range from the beginning tech with major airlines earning around $13.56 per hour, or about $27,120 per year, to $55,000-plus per year for the top 10 percent of technicians. Supervisors may top out in the $60,000 range. General aviation avionics personnel have an average salary range from $30,000 to $70,100. The number of aircraft, and thus the department size, has a considerable effect on general aviation salaries.

Employment Outlook

The forecast for the avionics technician for the next several years is excellent. There are about fifteen thousand such jobs nationwide right now. Because of the increased electronics use in modern aircraft, it is impossible for the A&P to keep up with the technology. The greatest need of the airlines at present is for bench-test qualified avionics personnel. These technicians actually disassemble the units and determine where the problems exist. One major carrier, however, requires that all A&P technicians hired have 750 hours of electronics/avionics experience, or appropriate schooling in lieu of experience.

Information from the industry tends to indicate that practically all graduates of avionics schools are offered jobs immediately. Refusing to relocate is about the only drawback to rapid employment in the avionics field. Most schools indicate a placement rate in the 90-percent range. Although the airlines seek experienced technicians, they will probably hire more workers directly from school as the crunch worsens. At present, general aviation and the larger avionics shops are the training grounds for most fresh graduates of avionics schools.

The Bottom Line

Avionics technicians are highly sought-after electronics specialists. The job outlook is positive. The working conditions are usually among the most desirable. Avionics technicians work in a variety of jobs not associated with airlines, which will be discussed in upcoming chapters. If you like mathematics and you can communicate well, avionics could provide an "electrifying" career.

Other Airline Positions

The airlines hire people with a diversity of expertise, education, and professional ability. Aside from the jobs already described in this chapter, there are far too many airline positions to list and define. One major airline lists more than 450 titled positions. Several of the positions have to do with the same major area of expertise, but they list different responsibilities within that field. An example would be that of an analyst. There are forty-six positions listed for this one skill. It is obvious that most analysts do similar things. In this case, they do it for different departments, thus creating forty-six different job classifications.

If you have a particular skill or some special knowledge, contact the airlines of your choice and find out whether it can use you in its lineup.

Canadian Airlines

Air Canada is the most visible Canadian carrier. The company added twelve Airbus 321 aircraft to its fleet in 2001. The carrier's cross-border routes with the United States are worth about $450 million per year to the airline. The bilateral agreement between the United States and Canada is as close to an "open-skies" agreement as the United States has with any nation. Canadian airlines have access to any U.S. airport. U.S. airlines have similar access in

Canada. (The United States' open-skies access to Toronto, Montreal, and Vancouver was complete by 1998. There are still some minor trade-related restrictions as of 2001.)

Canada as a whole requires about sixty-four thousand aviation maintenance workers. These workers earn from $28,000 to $54,000 a year, estimates the Canadian Aviation Maintenance Council. Canada had about fifty-one thousand licensed pilots in 2001. The Canadian air carrier fleet totals about six hundred big jets and regional passenger aircraft, according to the Air Transport Association of Canada.

3

AIRPORTS AND AIRFIELDS

THERE ARE MORE than 19,280 airports in the United States, of which 5,000 are public-use airports and the majority, more than 13,000, are private-use airports, according to the Federal Aviation Administration. An airport can be a grass strip located on a farm in Montana or an immense complex of concrete, metal, and people located in a major city. Fewer than seven hundred of our airports have scheduled air carrier service. General aviation airplanes serve the smaller airports. Approximately five thousand airports have a paved runway. Varying sizes and uses of airports require that those who operate them be of equal diversity.

A small airport may be a one-person operation or it may be a family business, affectionately referred to as a "mom-and-pop" operation. This type of airport is a dying breed for several reasons. The technology required for maintenance, flight training, charter, and other airport operations is changing so rapidly that Mom and Pop can no longer keep up. Many of the smaller operations are also being edged out by residential encroachment.

Numerous airports across the nation are permanently closed each year. FAA regulations are changing markedly, requiring safety fencing, costly environmental controls on storing fuel, and the ever-increasing paperwork, which leaves little time for taking care of the other things that must be accomplished.

The large airports may require thousands of employees to maintain a daily operation. The large airport is frequently compared to a small city. It has its own police force, fire department, maintenance crew, managers, stores, transportation system, parking lots, restaurants, even banks and places where businesspeople can obtain typing services, photocopies, and fax capability. For example, Chicago's O'Hare airport handled some sixty-seven million passengers in 2001. An operation of this magnitude must have some very specialized workers. Let's consider a few of them.

Airport Manager

The airport manager of a medium-sized airport must be experienced in several areas such as business management, civil engineering, personnel management, public relations, finance, and, of course, aviation. The very large airports will provide for a staff so that the special expertise is available through several assistants to the manager.

Education

The airport manager of just a few years ago probably came to the job in one of several ways: military service, which involved operating airfields; experience in directing a large fixed-base operation (FBO), a self-contained unit that provides a variety of services and usually is located in a medium-to-large airport; political appointment; or by working as an assistant to the manager of a medium-to-large airport.

Today an increasing number of airport managers are coming from colleges and universities that have programs specifically for educating the airport manager. Such courses of study are often found in the college's school of basic and applied sciences. The emphasis is on science, mathematics, computer science, and aviation management, with selected business courses in finance, human resource management, accounting, and marketing. It never hurts to have an additional course or two in psychology and public speaking.

The manager must defend budgets and expansion plans before the airport board. It is not uncommon for the manager to speak before civic clubs, visiting airport contingents, public forums concerned with noise from the airport, and other interested groups.

Certification

There is a special and very exclusive certification available for the airport manager who is skilled, experienced, and who will go through a rather long and very specific program of individual education. This program is available from the American Association of Airport Executives (AAAE) and allows a graduate to place the initials AAE after his or her name, much in the same manner as one who holds the doctorate. The certification is actually called accreditation and requires that the candidate have at least three years of airport management experience, write an original paper on some phase of airport management, and pass oral and written examinations on a level comparable to other professions. A four-year college degree, or its equivalent, is required. There are fewer than four hundred accredited airport executives in the United States.

Working Conditions

The airport manager is almost daily involved in enforcing airport and FAA rules and regulations, planning and supervising maintenance, and designing safety and security programs. The manager is also concerned with negotiating leases with airport tenants and airlines, programming future needs, developing budgets, promoting the use of the airport, training and supervising employees, and increasingly dealing with irate groups who are concerned with the noise from airports. It is a busy life and the work rarely dull.

Being an airport manager at medium and large airports is not an entry-level position. A person usually rises to this level by managing smaller airports or by working in the operations division of larger airports. One way to enter the operations department at many airports is through an internship while attending college. Numerous colleges, especially those with aviation programs, interact with airports to place students while they are in school. Some colleges have cooperative education programs with airports hundreds of miles from the campus. Students placed in these positions will live in the city where the airport is located for up to three semesters, working full-time at the airport.

The size of the airport and the specific title of the person will largely dictate whether he or she spends the majority of time indoors or outside. The young operations worker spends considerable time outside driving around runways and taxiways, perimeter fences, and other areas, checking on the condition of the airport. As experience is gained and more responsibility is assumed, the operations worker will tend to concentrate more time indoors.

Less than 10 percent of all airports are privately owned. A job in airport management is usually a job in public administration.

Once an entrepreneur, probably with flight experience, the airport manager today must be skilled in the governmental process and the business management of a public institution. Such an administrator will be first of all a professional, will be effective at problem solving, and will be politically sensitive.

Salary

Salaries of airport executives, like salaries for most positions, will vary with education, experience, and other qualifications, as well as being affected by the size and complexity of the hiring airport. Salary is also subject to geographic region, market forces, and local politics. Airports are divided into large, medium, and small hub airports as well as large, medium, and small nonhub airports for salary purposes. General aviation reliever airports form an additional segment of this career area.

Salaries for experienced managers will range from $18,000 to $181,000, depending on the above criteria. Executives at the largest airports may earn up to $200,000 annually. Managers at medium hub airports have an average salary of $92,000, with lesser positions averaging between $45,000 and $71,000. Small hub managers average $72,000. The managers at nonhub airports enjoy an average of $50,000.

Progressive experience is important to the hiring airport. Two to five years in an operations department, movement to deputy or assistant manager, and finally promotion to airport manager is the normal route to higher salaries. Many airport employees, due to the public nature of airports, will have fixed salaries, or a salary range that is dictated by specific years of previous related service. Such salaries are rarely open to negotiation. One of the principal publications that lists professional airport positions is the *Airport Report*, which goes to members of the American Association of Airport Executives.

More airports are hiring interns who are usually recent college graduates. These internships differ from the normal undergraduate internship in that the position is full-time and is usually for one year to eighteen months in duration. The full-time intern may receive a pay range of from $15,000 to $22,000 per year. Not all airports hire interns.

Employment Outlook

Due to the operating complexity of airports in today's environment, the job outlook for well-trained managers is positive. Every issue of *Airport Report* lists positions for airport managers. The majority of positions will obviously occur in states having the largest number of attended airports. States such as California, Texas, Florida, Illinois, New York, and Pennsylvania will have the greater number. Entry-level positions will occur in larger numbers at airports served by air carriers. The National Association of State Aviation Officials (NASAO) indicates that a definite need exists for college-educated airport planners and engineers. One may sometimes have to accept underemployment to break into airport management. The author knows one former student who spent a summer cutting grass at an airport in order to show his desire. He is now the operations director for that hub airport and has numerous subordinates reporting to him.

Airports contribute billions of dollars to the economy of the nation. Even community airports can be valuable assets to their local economies. A medium-sized airport in western Tennessee contributes more than $1.7 billion to the state economy in terms of wages, sales, taxes paid, and purchases made. Such airports operate twenty-four hours a day, seven days a week, and on holidays. Operations personnel, unlike some other airport workers, must be represented around-the-clock.

The Bottom Line

Airport management can provide a satisfying career, especially if you like working with people. The career provides a variety of experiences, with rarely a dull moment. Increasing complexity requires much more education than in previous years. With the tremendous growth in air carrier service since 1978, airports have become greatly congested both in the air overhead and on the ground. Innovative managers are needed to help solve the increasing problems. The pay is not as great as a comparably responsible position in the corporate world, but the excitement and the opportunity to be your own boss, to a certain degree, may compensate for lower salaries.

Fixed-Base Operator

The behind-the-scenes people who keep the planes flying are known in the industry as fixed-base operators. Commonly referred to as an FBO, or less often as a Flight Support Operator (FSO), a fixed-base operator fulfills a business function that is absolutely required for general aviation to survive. However, FBOs exist at all airports, not just general aviation airports. Thus, it is appropriate that we place the section on the FBO in the chapter about airports.

The typical FBO provides fuel, maintenance, flight instruction—and coffee. (Coffee is listed somewhat tongue-in-cheek as coffee sometimes becomes as important as fuel to the pilot and passenger!) An FBO may provide charter and air taxi services, crop dusting, aerial advertising, airplane rental, aircraft sales, and hangar rental. The larger FBO is becoming highly specialized and instead of offering the full range of services, may concentrate on refueling and executive services or may emphasize advanced airframe and engine technical services. Another FBO may specialize in interior renovation. Some FBOs provide late-baggage delivery service for airlines. Thus, one may readily see what some of the job possibilities are with FBOs. Most full-service FBOs operate 24 hours per day, 365 days per year.

The FBO may be a mom-and-pop operation at a small airfield, or it may be a large, multimillion-dollar operation utilizing the expert services of dozens of people. Several of the larger FBOs have established operations at numerous airports across the nation. Such companies often purchase an operating FBO and convert it to the name and operational directives of their other places. General aviation pilots become familiar with the services of these companies and tend to utilize them wherever they fly. Many FBOs also service major carrier airlines and commuter operations.

The Federal Aviation Administration (FAA) regulates practically every function of aviation. Each service provided by the FBO is regulated under one or more sections of the Federal Aviation Regulations. A person might create a position with an FBO simply by understanding the various regulations and being able to file the appropriate forms on behalf of the FBO. The future looks as though we may become more, rather than less, regulated. The FBO will also have to conform to the requirements of the airport at which it does business. Some airport authorities require that the FBO provide certain services in order to operate. Typical offerings are flight instruction, fuel, maintenance, and aircraft storage.

Education

FBOs vary so much in size and personnel that it is difficult to discuss their employment needs and educational requirements. In the past, many young people started a career in aviation by working for an FBO in exchange for flight time. Those days are almost gone, due in large part to federal regulations concerned with minimum wages, child labor laws, and all of the restrictions regarding such factors as social security, income tax deductions, and hazardous working conditions. An occasional FBO may still be willing to hire workers without a specialty or skill to do odd jobs like cleanup, fueling, and washing aircraft. The educational level for such workers may be less than high school. However, that is becoming rare as well.

Today the typical FBO will hire maintenance technicians, pilot/instructors, secretaries, marketing personnel, and—depending upon the size of the operation—dispatchers and charter pilots. The educational level of such workers will vary from one FBO to another. Some may be college-educated. Others may have specialized schooling beyond high school that does not include a college degree.

Certification

Certification applies to the pilots and maintenance technicians. Special qualifications may also apply to the chief pilot and dispatchers. The FAA regulates all such certification.

Working Conditions

Working conditions vary from one FBO to another. Several of the "chain" FBOs have multimillion dollar physical plants. Million Air has twenty-seven units in its network. Signature Flight Support Corp., Orlando, Florida, which came into being from the consolidation of three well-known FBOs—Page Avjet, Butler, and Van Dusen—operates some forty-three units in the United States and five overseas. Signature acquired AMR Combs in 1999, after agreeing to the terms of a Justice Department antitrust settlement. Combs had eleven units and its Denver location was voted the number one FBO in the United States for fifteen consecutive years. That is a record that is not likely to be surpassed.

The type of FBO being opened today is light-years away from the facilities of the past. Fort Lauderdale Jet Center opened in late 1989 and is somewhat typical of what we will see in the future. Its terminal covers 120,000 square feet and comes complete with pilot's lounge, sleeping room, sauna, gym, and showers. The center has three conference rooms, audiovisual equipment for meetings, rental cars, a gift shop, catering services, and a shuttle to the airline terminal. U.S. customs and agriculture inspection stations are located next door. There are twelve acres of ramp space and thirty-six thousand square feet of hangar space, with more in the planning stages.

Compare that description with the old FBO that consisted of maybe ten thousand square feet, in which planes were stored and worked on, with one dirty bathroom used by everyone. An attached lean-to formed a business office, containing a desk, the typical clock inset into a wooden propeller, and a few greasy rags that the owner/mechanic left on frequent trips from the hangar. Although you see a very different future for most of the FBOs, the old-style FBO is not extinct. Many an airline captain, corporate jet pilot, and general aviation mechanic have great memories left over from the FBOs of yesteryear.

Nevertheless, the clear wave of the future is toward more specialized FBOs. Although these new FBOs might lack some of the nostalgic appeal of the smaller, mom-and-pop FBOs of the past, they will be better positioned to thrive in an increasingly competitive, service-oriented market.

Your working conditions will be different from what they may have been ten years ago. The FBO of today has competition. The name of the game is consistent, fast, and courteous service. Many people may initially be attracted to a glittering facility with lots of extras. However, unless the service aspect is also available, they will not likely remain long. Repeat customers are a must and service is what brings them back.

Salary

There is a long-standing joke about FBOs that begins with a question: Do you know how to make a small fortune in aviation? Yes, go into the FBO business with a large fortune. This may be nearer the truth than we would like to believe. Even on the airfield where only one FBO has a monopoly business, it is at risk due to a large number of events. The basic economy affects aviation to a greater degree than it does most businesses. It is sometimes difficult to find competent and hardworking employees. High fuel prices can hit at the wrong time. New aircraft sales, especially in the training market, have been almost nonexistent in recent years. Environmental regulation, as it relates to buried fuel tanks, is of major concern and is quite costly to the FBO. Insurance, employee benefits, rising salaries, and the equipment necessary to maintain the more complex aircraft all increase the FBO's expenses.

Thus, salaries offered by your local FBO may be quite different from those offered a few states away. Rates of pay for the various kinds of jobs found at FBOs are detailed in Chapter 5, on general aviation.

Employment Outlook

Civil aviation did not have its best years in the last decade of the twentieth century. Light aircraft manufacturing was greatly diminished in volume in the United States and FBOs were closing at a rapid rate. A glut of pilots and maintenance technicians appeared when several major airlines closed their doors. Flight instruction had been depressed, with fewer student starts owing to the recession, the rising cost of instruction, increasing fuel costs, and fewer places to find quality instruction. Although there are still almost four thousand FBOs, the skills needed to work in them are changing. The nation is moving away from production and into service-oriented business. The FBO is certainly a service business. In addition to FAA certification for those positions requiring it, one also needs to have a service philosophy to find work at today's FBO.

The Bottom Line

The FBO is changing. Perhaps you can be part of that change. If you like working with people, being around airplanes, and being the best at what you do, the FBO provides such an opportunity. Thousands of airports nationwide have one or more fixed-base operators. They need all kinds of motivated people to assist in the operation of their businesses. Many are increasing their base into large charter operations. Some are involved in maintaining and refurbishing fleets of executive jet aircraft. Others supply fuel to the major air carriers. Many repair both the most complex jet and the smallest, single-engine training airplane, virtually side-by-side. If you meet the personal criteria listed above, you certainly have a place with the FBO.

One sad commentary on FBOs is that they are slowly dwindling. There were ten thousand FBOs in the United States in 1980. That number was reduced to four thousand in 1998, and it is anticipated that there may be no more than two thousand needed in the twenty-first century.

Other Airport Careers

You can see that the airport is often as diverse as a medium-sized city. As such, a variety of careers are available to accommodate almost every level of education and professional expertise. The airport needs workers in the major categories of craft trades, including craftsmen like electricians, plumbers, and carpenters. People with backgrounds in accounting, finance, human relations, and civil engineering are utilized. Noise abatement officers and airport planners are also specialty careers. In addition, emergency services personnel such as firefighters, police officers, and paramedics are required. Finally, maintenance workers, skycaps, clerks, restaurant workers, and concessionaire employees can find airport jobs. Some of these workers are employed by outside contractors instead of by the airport. However, the airport personnel office usually can advise you of positions in those categories.

4

ENGINEERING RESEARCH AND DEVELOPMENT

RESEARCH AND DEVELOPMENT (R&D) activities occur in three primary places: in universities, within the major industrial corporations, and within governmental agencies, including the various branches of the military. R&D activities are considered separately for the reason that R&D becomes the workplace. There are also many similarities in education, job function, and the manner in which researchers come to their positions.

The aerospace industry conducts more R&D than nearly any other industry. R&D also is a major contributor to the economic health of the nation. Without it, the country remains static and thus falls behind other nations in technological progress. The United States has been the leader in air carrier aircraft development since the beginning of aviation. The nation also leads in space development for commercial purposes and has practically been the sole supplier of general aviation aircraft and components. Some of this is changing, with the entry of Japan and Europe into the space market and with Airbus making considerable inroads into the air carrier market. A good aerospace engineer can work almost anywhere in the world that he or she chooses.

R&D Specialist

People involved in R&D activities come from many fields of learning. The majority tend to come from engineering, mathematics, or the sciences. Engineers apply the sciences in the work they perform. Engineering has developed primarily within the past two hundred years, with more than one hundred specialized engineering branches today.

Education

The education of an R&D specialist should begin early in life, certainly by the time he or she enters high school. Four years of mathematics, with advanced courses where possible, are required. You should take all of the science courses offered in high school, especially the physical science courses. Communication skills also are absolutely necessary. You should begin to become familiar with computer languages at an early stage of development. If courses such as logic and reasoning are available, enroll in them. Do lots of reading, especially critical analyses and biographies of famous scientists and innovators in all areas. One or more foreign languages can be useful.

College brings the real commitment to intensive study. The first year is normally one of meeting general studies requirements. The sophomore year can be one of further exploration among the sciences and engineering. You should select a particular science, or the discipline of engineering, for concentration by the end of the sophomore year. Electives may be chosen in other sciences outside the major. A double major of science and mathematics could be a good choice.

Graduate school is a must for the researcher. However, recent studies of science fields suggest that one may be perceived as overqualified when there is an overabundance of scientists. Further concentration in the major, deeper study into the elements of research, and anything that will assist you in independent thinking should be a part of the one to three years of graduate study. A master's degree normally may be obtained within a calendar year. With hard work and excellent planning, the doctorate may be added within two additional years.

Working Conditions

The majority of a researcher's work takes place in the laboratory. Of course, the laboratory may be somewhat different in aerospace than in other areas. The researcher may be working in huge wind tunnels, in engine test facilities that would dwarf some factories, or at test ranges where rockets and supersonic engines are given final approval.

Many researchers do work in the traditional laboratory environment of chemicals, test tubes, ovens, and weird-sounding paraphernalia. They design new composites for airfoils, engines for hypersonic flight, flame-resistant materials for the interior of airplanes, and weapons systems for jet fighters. More recent developments in R&D include microelectronics, superconductivity, and robotics.

Salary

There is a tremendous variation in salaries, even within the professional R&D ranks. Salary profiles are closely related to educational level, years of experience, and the discipline within R&D that you have chosen to pursue. Table 4.1 shows median salaries of R&D specialists by discipline.

Salaries in R&D range from fewer than $15,000 to more than $90,000 per year. Due to the late acceptance of women into R&D, their salaries tend to cluster closer at the lower end of the professional scale.

Looking strictly at the aerospace engineer profession in the year 2000, salaries vary by specialty. A big new project will cause a shift in the pay structure. A new commercial airliner such as Boeing's sonic cruiser may attract talent with high pay; or the joint strike fighter project by Lockheed and partners may need to staff up and therefore will recruit heavily. Table 4.2 shows an industry-wide breakdown of salary levels. Remember that these are just averages.

Educational level is a factor in the salary of most careers. Careers not affected by educational level tend to be those in fields with strong unionization or ones where seniority—length of service—determines salary and other benefits. Even within those careers, a

Table 4.1 A Comparison of Engineering Specialties

Engineering Specialty	2001 Hourly Wage
Petroleum engineers	$43.02
Nuclear engineers	$34.60
Chemical engineers	$33.37
Mining engineers	$32.66
Aerospace engineers	$30.96
Electrical/electronics engineers	$30.35
Materials engineers	$27.28
Mechanical engineers	$26.26
Industrial engineers	$25.26

Source: Reed/Elsevier, *Design News* 2001

Table 4.2 Salaries of Aerospace Engineers, by Specialties and Educational Level

New Hires	
Bachelor's degree, aerospace engineering	$46,918
Master's degree, aerospace engineering	$59,955
Ph.D. candidates, aerospace engineering	$64,167
Experienced Engineers	
Federal government	$74,170
Search and navigation equipment	$71,020
Aircraft and parts	$68,230
Guided missiles, space vehicles, and parts	$65,830

Source: U.S. Bureau of Labor Statistics, 2000 survey, and 2001 salary survey by the National Association of Colleges and Employers

higher educational level may assist you in initially being hired over less-educated workers.

Holding a doctorate makes a lifetime difference of nearly $1 million over the master's degree. And what if you do not obtain a degree at all? The person with the earned doctorate is estimated to have a career benefit in excess of $3 million, or nearly $86,000 per year, over the person in R&D who does not obtain any degree. Earning a degree is not for everyone. It doesn't make one less of a person not to have a degree. However, if you are capable of earning a degree, more especially a graduate degree, your career earning power is multiplied several times.

Employment Outlook

The Bureau of Labor Statistics (BLS) projects an improving climate for scientists and engineers by the year 2000. Aerospace engineers, of whom there are around fifty thousand in the United

States, are in a profession that is growing again. The growth prospects are based on the production of new civilian aircraft and renewed defense spending.

The aerospace industry is a labor-intensive industry that usually employs as many salaried workers as production workers. This is unusual among manufacturing industries. The aerospace industry employs somewhere in the vicinity of 20 percent of all scientists and engineers in the United States. Females account for around 8 percent of all aerospace engineers. About one in ten aerospace engineers is employed with federal agencies.

The Bottom Line

The position of research and development offers the opportunity to explore, innovate, create, and develop to the limits of your own capabilities. It affords a comfortable living, a pleasant working environment, and the opportunity to interact with other researchers to produce the finest aerospace products in the world.

Technical Change

Working within a highly technical area requires that you remain up to date. If you work for a company that falls behind, the industry can pass right by and make that company obsolete. You must assume individual responsibility for keeping up in technical matters. Participating in professional associations, attending national and international conferences, reading broadly, and interacting with colleagues frequently will keep you on the cutting edge of technology.

5

GENERAL AVIATION

GENERAL AVIATION (GA) is more a concept than a workplace. It includes almost all of aviation except the military and the airlines, thus encompassing a huge segment of American aviation. If the skies look crowded sometimes, it might be because there are an estimated 225,000 active GA aircraft in the United States. Of these, 78 percent—around 175,000—are piston-engine airplanes. Of the 22 percent remaining, 3 percent are turboprop planes, that is, they have a jet engine geared to a propeller. Another 4 percent are turbojet airplanes, sometimes called pure jet aircraft. Around 4 percent are rotorcraft, such as helicopters, that are supported in flight by rotating airfoils. That leaves around 11 percent, which falls into the "other" category, with experimental craft and additional classifications too numerous to list.

There are some 625,600 active licensed pilots in the United States, with about 6 percent being female. Approximately 117,000 pilots hold the air transport certificate (ATP), which is required of most airline pilots. Women hold about 2.3 percent of these certificates. The number of new pilot "starts"—that is, new students who are seeking to become pilots—has been declining annually since 1983. There is hope that this figure will increase due to special programs started by several GA organizations, as well as the fact that Congress made flight training a permanent part of the GI Bill in 1994. Military veterans may obtain 60 percent of their flight training costs from the Veterans Administration (VA), up to $14,000, after paying for the private pilot certificate on their own.

In Canada approximately fifty-one thousand individuals hold some type of pilot license, which may range from the private license for helicopters and fixed-wing through balloons, ultralights, gliders, and airline transport licenses. About nine thousand individuals hold the airline transport license or some 16 percent of license holders. This compares favorably with about 18 percent of U.S. pilots who hold this highest certificate. Females hold slightly over 5 percent of Canadian pilot licenses and around 2 percent hold the airline transport license, which also compares favorably with U.S. female pilots.

U.S. aircraft fly some forty-one million hours annually. GA aircraft fly nearly 59 percent of these hours. Air carriers fly 85 percent of the passengers transported in the United States. However, the airlines also use 95 percent of the aviation fuel consumed in this country. Of the more than 18,000 landing facilities in the United States, airlines serve only 670 of them. This leaves GA to serve 96 percent of all landing facilities.

GA, then, is a major contributor to the national economy and to the local economy in communities where a GA airport is located. This chapter will further define GA, describe many of its needs for skilled and professional workers, and yield information as to how you can enter the exciting world of general aviation.

Divisions of General Aviation

General aviation is made up of several distinct divisions. GA flying is divided as follows:

1. business flying
2. executive flying
3. commercial flying
4. personal flying
5. instructional flying

Business flying consists of aircraft personally flown in the conduct of business, but not for compensation or hire. For example, if a person sells heavy equipment and if that person flies around the state or region talking with construction companies, state and local highway departments, and other users of bulldozers and graders, that activity is classified as business flying.

Executive flying occurs when companies transport their top officers, employees, or goods by air and use professional pilots to operate their aircraft.

Commercial flying is divided into several segments such as air taxi, rental aircraft, aerial application, and others.

Personal flying is just what it sounds like. A person owns or rents an airplane for transportation, for the sheer fun of flying, or perhaps even to show the airplane in competition with others.

Instructional flying utilizes an airplane to teach others how to fly. This may be, as described by a friend, William Kershner, a one-airplane/one-person/one sick-sack operation, or it can be a large school with dozens of airplanes and instructors. General aviation instruction customarily falls in between these extremes.

Business Aircraft Use

There are few aviation-related jobs in companies wherein the owner utilizes an airplane to conduct the business of that company. You may become an accountant or a salesperson or have some other skill, plus a private pilot's certificate, and fly as part of that business. The difference is that you are flying on behalf of the business, not flying for hire for that company. You may not fly for hire unless you have at least a commercial certificate and instrument rating.

There is a tremendous amount of business flying in the United States. However, most such flying does not involve a flight department or the need for aviation-related personnel. Aircraft utilized in business flying are normally maintained by a fixed-base operator (FBO) and do not require crewing. Although some aircraft are sophisticated jets and turboprops, the majority are light, single-engine airplanes that carry four to six persons on flights of approximately four hours duration. The famous golfer Arnold Palmer would be an example of a business flyer who has his own jet airplane and jet helicopter. He also operates an aviation-related business, in addition to flying himself to golf tournaments.

Executive Flying

One of the most interesting areas of general aviation is that of executive flight. Even though it accounts for only 11 percent of all GA flying, it affords one of the greatest opportunities for employment. Executive flight requires professional pilots, maintenance crews, and—depending upon the size of the operation—flight schedulers, flight attendants, and managers of the flight and maintenance operations.

Why Executive Aircraft?

There are those who believe that flying corporate executives by private jet or turboprop airplane is pampering them beyond reason, in addition to the high salaries often paid to such executives. Nothing could be further from the truth. There are several reasons for using executive aircraft. Chief among them is saving the executive's time; in some cases it's also a matter of protection from possible threats.

Time wasted in airports waiting for an airliner, sitting on the runway waiting for twenty jets ahead of you to take off, and circling in holding patterns above an airport while waiting for better weather or clearance to land is not productive time for the top executives of corporations. These are among the pitfalls of executive travel on airlines. Now consider how much better the executive's time can be spent aboard a corporate jet, in conference with others in the company while moving directly from the home airport to the destination airport at 520 miles per hour.

The most modern company jet has a computer, fax machine, VCR/TV, even broadband Internet, a secretarial workstation, and full galley (kitchen) on board. These are comforts, true, yet they all save the time of a busy decision-maker, enhancing that executive's worth to the company. Corporate jets carry from five to eighteen persons, depending upon the type of plane. There are other factors that are also important to the executive. Mental alertness and increased physical stamina—as compared to fatigue from flying the airlines, reduction in overnight stays away from home, and an improved work environment en route—all are good reasons for using the executive aircraft.

You might expect that the United States would have the largest fleet of executive aircraft, and it does. Approximately 70 percent of the world's executive fleet belong to American corporations. This provides many job opportunities for you. And, if you become certified and experienced with corporate-type aircraft, you have the opportunity to work on similar aircraft in other countries for today's global corporations. This is a very good way to see the world.

The two leading producers of executive jets are Cessna, with several models of the Citation, and Learjet, with an equal number of different models. Coming on strong are Gulfstream, with the absolute top-of-the-line jet, and Dassault, which makes the Falcon 7x jet and several other models, a couple of them with three engines. Believe it or not, some multinational corporations operate airliner-type aircraft, and some wealthy individuals also own personal jets of the size and type that major carriers fly.

Job Outlook

Corporations provide an excellent opportunity for the professional pilot and the maintenance technician in particular. Other positions are possible, such as flight attendant, flight department manager, and maintenance technician assistant. However, flight attendant positions are often "on-call" positions with little stability. Managers often rise from pilot or maintenance positions and are rarely hired directly to manage an operation. Other positions are possible but will require persistence.

Finding a corporate position is often more difficult than getting a job with an airline or a fixed-base operator. There is less turnover in the corporate field. One of the best ways to obtain a corporate position is by referral and by having experience on the type of aircraft in the corporate fleet.

Many corporations have helicopters in addition to jet and turboprop airplanes. The corporate helicopter is taking on many of the characteristics of the plush corporate jet. Many models are heavily soundproofed and have leather seats, telephones, small bars, and fold-out worktables. Some executive helicopters sell for as much as $6 million. The helicopter market took a nosedive, so to speak, in the early 1980s, due to the energy crunch. Revival of the industry began in 1987 and has continued somewhat erratically since. The helicopter has the greatest opportunity for growth of any part of the transportation industry, assuming we can solve the major problems of high maintenance costs and the lack of public heliports in convenient locations.

There are many hidden job opportunities here. Petroleum Helicopters, Inc. of Lafayette, Louisiana, operates some 280 aircraft and employs 600 pilots. International hiring can be good if one can handle the rigors of living in some unusual places. For example, one company has need of helicopters, pilots, and mechanics in a Heli-skiing operation in British Columbia.

Salaries

Rates of pay in executive aviation vary by experience, certificates held, geographic region of the nation, and size and financial strength of the particular company. Other factors contribute to salary, though not as significantly as those listed above.

Salaries of general aviation pilots who transport executives are, in most cases, considerably lower than salaries for comparable positions with many airlines. Some corporations, however, will impose more stringent requirements for applicants than will the major carrier airlines.

Not everyone wants to fly for the airlines. Many pilots enjoy taking the same passengers on the majority of their flights. They become aware of expectations, where they will be going on most flights, who maintains their airplane, what the peculiar characteristics are of the plane they fly regularly, and how financially stable the company is. There are perks in both the air carrier and GA arenas of flight.

Captains for corporations had a median (figure that separates the top half from the bottom half) salary in 2000 of $72,673, according to a National Business Aviation Association (NBAA) salary survey. Depending upon the type of aircraft flown, the median salary ranged from $53,000 for turboprop airplanes to $88,500 for heavy jets. Median salaries were highest in the eastern region of the United States. Pharmaceutical companies paid a slightly higher average salary than other types of companies.

Copilots received a median salary in 1998 of $42,000 per year. Less was offered for single-engine planes and more for heavy jets. Companies in the western Pacific region offered the highest salaries. The chemical industry paid copilots slightly higher salaries than did other industries.

Aviation Department Managers

Managers of aviation departments are often senior captains who have stopped flying on a regular basis, or pilots who are still active and who assume managerial duties along with flying. The median base salary for managers in 1999 was $80,950. The East had the highest average salaries among the various regions. Pharmaceutical companies again led the industry in highest average salaries for this category—$126,000.

The aviation department manager is something of a new breed of pilot in today's complex GA environment. The manager must have leadership qualities, normally vast experience as a pilot, ability to compare the several models of aircraft within the category the company can afford, computer literacy, financial responsibility, and capability to meet the demands of "super" executives within a highly competitive atmosphere. In short, the manager must have many of the same qualities that the senior officers of the corporations have.

Chief Pilot

A job that calls for the skills of both manager and pilot is chief pilot. In some smaller companies, the same person may be the aviation department manager and the senior pilot. Job responsibilities that tend to define this person's position differently from that of the department manager have to do mainly with training. The chief pilot plans and implements the pilot training program of other company pilots, acts as the manager in the absence of the department manager, and may select and terminate pilots. The chief pilot may maintain the files of pilot currency and medical examinations as well as interacting with the FAA on pilot proficiency checks. The chief pilot may, in the absence of a company chief of maintenance, also be responsible for coordinating the maintenance technicians.

The chief pilot, of which there were more than five hundred responding to the 2000 NBAA survey, had a median annual base salary in 1999 of $80,000. The range varied from those pilots at the smallest companies, flying light twin-engine planes, who earned a median salary of $68,175, to the jet chief pilot with a median salary of $106,250. The eastern region of the United

States was slightly ahead of the other regions, and the pharmaceutical industry tended to award higher salaries to chief pilots.

Other Aviation-Related Positions

Other workers found in executive aviation departments are flight attendants, with a median annual base salary of $38,900; the chief of maintenance, $64,700; the A&P technician, $47,000; the maintenance technician helper, $25,875; and the scheduler and dispatcher, $34,320. Flight engineers, sometimes known as the third pilot, commanded a salary of $61,600. Flight engineers are found almost exclusively in companies with heavy jet aircraft. These salaries were current in 1998–99.

Keep in mind that there is considerable difference among salaries paid in relationship to the size of the company, the type of aircraft on which pilots and technicians are qualified, the location of the company, whether the company flies international routes, and the business in which the company is engaged. The size of the department, the number of aircraft flown, the years of experience of the individual, and the income of the company also affect salaries. The best time to conduct research on the company for which you wish to work is while you are training for the type of position you want to perform. The more you know about that company, or the region in which you wish to be employed, the more likely you are to be hired.

Salary is important, but it is by no means the only item to consider. You must be happy where you are working. You must have a philosophy that is in keeping with the type of company for which you wish to work. You will not be happy working for a chemical or petroleum company if you are a dedicated environmentalist. You might think ahead about raising a family and the type of environment in which you wish that to take place. Planning can rarely be overdone. You can always take advantage of serendipity should the opportunity arise.

Some of the perks of flying executive aircraft have to do with the sophistication of the airplanes. Some of the heavy executive jets like the Gulfstream, the Falcon 900, and the Canadair Challenger, sell for up to $30 million. They have every state-of-the-art navigation device known. The more recent models have the "glass cockpit," a series of cathode ray tubes that display computer-generated symbols and information. The glass cockpit is replacing the rapidly disappearing engine and navigation instruments of older aircraft. The computers may be programmed to actually fly the airplane and keep the pilots advised of problems. Computers monitor much of the maintenance. The airplanes have speeds approaching Mach 1 (650 knots per hour at sea level), and they include most of the comforts of home.

Additional perks come in the form of international travel, vacations at resorts owned by the corporation, and the opportunity to meet captains of industry as well as public figures and celebrities who may have occasion to travel aboard company jets. Life within the corporate structure may be just what you seek.

Commercial Aviation

Commercial aviation is difficult to define, in the sense that it encompasses such a wide variety of activities. Some of the flying is that which a fixed-base operator (FBO), as described in Chapter 3, may provide. Some of it falls into a category called charter and air taxi, which is often confused in terminology with small regional air carriers. Much of commercial aviation involves activities that are little known to the general public. This section will briefly describe some of the activities of commercial aviation but will not delve into the salaries and working conditions. You can get a general feel for these factors by reviewing the sections in Chapter 3 concerning pilots and technicians.

Commercial aviation is made up of three divisions:

1. air taxi/charter operations
2. rental use
3. aerial application and other uses

Air taxi operations involve any air carrier certified by the FAA that carries passengers for hire and meets specified minimum equipment regulations for flying in marginal weather conditions. The normal air taxi will operate over rather limited geographic areas, often within state boundaries.

Charter operators may function locally or may range all over the United States. These operators are normally certified under FAA Regulation Part 135, and they fly everything from nuts and bolts, to bodies, passengers, and bank checks. The general public is not aware how much banking depends on aviation. Billions of dollars worth of checks wend their way by car or truck to a nearby local airport, are placed into a light, single-engine airplane, and then are flown to a larger central airport to meet other planes. The checks are then loaded into a larger and faster jet to be flown to a location where up to a dozen or more jets will congregate, exchange checks, and do a reverse of the earlier operation. Such activity not only means great amounts of money to the banking industry, but it also provides numerous jobs for the aviation industry.

Rental use involves airplanes of all types, from the smallest trainer to large, multiengine turboprops. The majority of rental aircraft are those utilized in flight training. However, there are many qualified pilots who do not choose to own an airplane and who must rent an airplane for whatever purpose they choose to fly. Additional information on rentals may be found under the sections on FBOs in Chapter 3 and flight instruction later in this chapter.

Aerial application is often called crop dusting, a reference to aerial spraying of pesticides over farm crops. It involves much more. Greater use of the airplane is being made for planting crops as well as controlling pests. Other commercial uses can involve patrolling of pipelines and power lines, wildlife surveys, photography and aerial mapping, spotting for commercial fishing fleets, fire fighting, and various police activities. The future of commercial aviation looks positive. It should grow with increased flexibility of aircraft development. Helicopters will come into wider and more popular use.

When considering your career in commercial aviation, you will begin by following one of the traditional routes to FAA certification, such as maintenance or pilot preparation, or by preparing yourself in an area that can be utilized within the aviation industry. Some colleges offer special programs that combine flight and agricultural expertise. Others offer independent departments of aviation and criminal justice, so that you can combine flight with law enforcement. A little research on your part will yield several combinations that can make you valuable to commercial aviation.

There is a subcategory that does not exactly fit the above classifications. It involves the use of aircraft in law enforcement. Helicopters are in particular demand. The Airborne Law Enforcement Association comprises more than 360 member agencies that own some eight hundred helicopters. Of the agencies responding to a 1994 survey, 64 percent operate only turbine aircraft. Around

21 percent fly a mix of piston and turbine engines. The police helicopter is usually equipped in a very sophisticated way with forward-looking infrared (FLIR), night-vision goggles, Loran C, and multifrequency radios. Some 64 percent of the respondents also operate fixed-wing aircraft. Pilots for law enforcement agencies average salaries in the high $30,000 category.

Personal Aviation

U.S. pilots log several million hours of personal flying—that is, flying for pleasure—each year. Such flying can range from a couple of hours with the family on a Sunday afternoon, to one of the more than five hundred yearly flights by light aircraft across the Atlantic Ocean. Personal flying may take place in a one-hundred-horsepower, single-engine, fixed-gear, two-place (two-seat) aircraft, or it may be in a Korean War vintage F-86 Supersabre fighter at speeds in excess of six hundred miles per hour. Whatever the reason or the type of aircraft used, personal flying can be satisfying and beneficial. If you are interested in flying, but choose not to make a career of it, you may still wish to become a private pilot and own or rent an airplane for pleasure. Female pilots account for about 6 percent of all U.S. pilots. Studies of flight safety statistics indicate that women in GA have proportionately fewer accidents than do men.

Instructional Flying

All pilot astronauts, fighter pilots for the armed forces, captains of major airlines, and aerobatics pilots at air shows began their flying at the same point—with zero experience. Not all went through the same type of training program. Not all flew the same type of aircraft in the beginning, and certainly each did not have the same motivation. Yet, they all began flying as we began life—at the "front end."

The front end for most pilots is a small-to-medium-sized airport, a two-place, single-engine airplane, and a young flight instructor with perhaps three hundred to nine hundred hours of flight experience. For the military pilot-to-be, instruction may actually begin in a small jet, but the basics are still there. So when you stand in awe of the major airline captain who commands a giant Boeing 747, just remember, she or he got started in the same way you will have to begin.

Flight instruction is often a means of "building time." Even with flight certificates and ratings abundantly available in your purse or billfold, you'd better have a minimum number of hours of actual flight time, or few employers will hire you as a pilot. One of the ways to obtain that all-important time is to instruct others in the art and science of flying. This not only helps to build time, but it also gives you some return on the investment of money already put into your own training.

A flight instructor may earn from $7 to $15 per hour for teaching in light aircraft and perhaps as much as $25 for multiengine instruction. The instructor providing turboprop or other specialized instruction may earn even more. These are often salaried positions, and some pay very well.

There are professional flight instructors out there somewhere, but they are difficult to locate. They can stand to instruct only so many hours per day, due to the fatigue of teaching neophyte pilots. The airplane cockpit is not a good classroom. It is often noisy, filled with sunshine, tense due to surrounding traffic, and contains a student who may not know what to do next. The mental alertness required of the instructor can be overwhelming. The majority of instructors begin to burn out within a year or two and yearn for other types of flying. If you find a longtime professional from whom to take instruction, consider yourself a fortunate person indeed.

Qualifications for Canadian flight instructors are considerably more demanding than are those for instructors in the United States. Canada has a multilevel tier of instruction certificates, wherein the lower levels must work under the supervision of higher-level instructors.

Flight instruction cannot take place without numerous other services being available. Fuel, hangars, maintenance, airport management, and related services are found where instruction is given. That means jobs for you, if you are interested in general aviation. Spend some time at an airport and observe what happens. You may find your niche in aviation there.

Airplane Sales

Everyone is familiar with automobile dealerships and used car lots. The newspapers and television bombard us daily with advertising about the great deals we can get down at "Crazy Ernie's Car Emporium." However, you've probably never seen an ad for "Lucky Lindy's Plane Plaza!" Few of us realize the extent to which airplane sales are a major part of the aviation environment.

When you give it some thought, you realize that someone has to sell the hundreds of airplanes that are being manufactured each year. You now know that we are speaking of airplanes that may cost anywhere from $4,000 to $150 million and up. We will confine our comments primarily to general aviation aircraft. Although the companies that build the F-16, the B-747, and the fast attack helicopter must also have sales representatives, these are rather specialized areas with limited job opportunities. Your best chance of being involved in airplane sales will come from general aviation.

Education

There are no specified levels of education required for a career in airplane sales. However, you need to be able to deal effectively with the kind of person with whom you come in contact. Will you be selling a small, two-place trainer to the blue-collar worker who always wanted to learn to fly and can now afford to do so? Or will you be showing a new Ag-Cat crop duster to a farmer? How about a $23-million Gulfstream IV to the owner of a major manufacturing company? What do you emphasize with each person? What kind of items do you believe will impress them? Your educational background can make a difference.

Working Conditions

Working conditions in airplane sales will vary considerably. There are two basic workplaces for the airplane sales representative. One is with the manufacturer, selling either from the factory or within the dealer organization in the field. The other is with a company that specializes in selling used aircraft. There will be some similarities. Both sales reps will be on the phone quite a lot, looking for prospects. The factory representative may receive more calls about the purchase of airplanes than the used aircraft counterpart. Some sales reps are constantly looking for used airplanes either to buy for resale or to list in their inventory. There are several high-quality magazines and news sources that exclusively list airplanes for sale.

The factory representative accompanies airplanes to major trade shows like the National Business Aviation Association (NBAA) meeting held each year. This show usually attracts about seventeen thousand people from around the world. This is "big sale" time. Some used aircraft companies also send aircraft to this type of show. The static display consists of dozens of airplanes worth millions of dollars.

Salaries

You probably would assume that there is a difference between the person selling a small Cessna and one selling a Falcon 900. There is! A good salesperson can make a fine salary selling either. However, it stands to reason that the small-aircraft representative will have to sell quite a few more airplanes to make the same amount of money as the jet salesperson. In fact, the person selling the top-of-the-line jet likely will not sell more than five per year. The jet sales rep may earn an annual base salary from $30,000 to $50,000 or more, plus maybe $16,000 per plane in commission. The total compensation can easily reach over $100,000. Straight commission is the best deal, provided you are good at this business and can survive for a month or so without a sale.

Employment Outlook

The sales community is always looking for good sales representatives. You don't even have to possess a pilot's certificate, although it will enhance your opportunity for a job and for a sale if you do.

You will probably have to start small and build your reputation. There are international opportunities as well as those in the United States. You also can find some good flight opportunities with the ferry companies that transport the airplane to the buyer. Some of those go to Australia and many to Europe. Any FBO that has a dealership may help you learn how to begin. Or ask at the FBO to see a copy of the advertising literature on airplane sales.

The Bottom Line

You first have to decide if you want to sell, fly, or make a lot of money. You may combine these, but you need to know your motivation. Airplane sales is a very competitive business, and you will feel like you are in a pressure cooker all the time. Some people thrive on such an atmosphere. Others burn out quickly. Your motivation will have some effect on which happens to you.

Learn as much as you can about airplanes. Know engines, avionics, and performance standards. Learn relative prices. Know FAA directives. Know your aircraft—the good ones and the flaws of models that are "dogs." If you do your homework, you will receive the rewards.

Other General Aviation Flying

Each year, five thousand aircraft and more than nine hundred thousand hours of flight go into this category. It includes aircraft flown in support of aircraft sales, research, glider towing, and parachuting. Other uses are as diverse as you are innovative in thinking of ways to use aircraft. Further reading in the books listed in Appendix B will help you decide on a career in general aviation.

The Advanced General Aviation Transport Experiments, or AGATE, which is an eight-year, $63 million, government-industry-academia project, was launched in 1994. The program focus is on developing single-pilot, light, all weather, and transportation aircraft using new technology for crashworthiness, composite materials, low-cost propellers, simpler propulsion, icing protection, and other safety enhancing developments. By 2001 the AGATE general aviation propulsion (GAP) project had developed an improved propeller/engine integration design and a new jet engine prototype among other projects. GA seems to be a fertile field for applying advances in automatic control theory as well.

6

GOVERNMENT AVIATION

THE FEDERAL GOVERNMENT hires thousands of people to work in aviation-related positions. The Federal Aviation Administration (FAA) is the largest employer of civilians working in aviation within the federal employment system. Other positions are associated with such agencies as the National Aeronautics and Space Administration (NASA); the Civil Air Patrol (CAP), a civilian auxiliary of the U.S. Air Force; the National Transportation Safety Board (NTSB); the U.S. Customs Service; and the Defense Mapping Agency.

Federal positions pay among the highest salaries, have an excellent retirement plan, normally involve working conditions that are pleasant, and provide excellent fringe benefits. Continuing education opportunities and generous vacation accumulation are among such benefits. The added advantage is that you also serve your country while earning a comfortable living.

Federal Aviation Administration (FAA)

The Federal Aviation Administration (FAA) is charged with the regulation of civil aviation in the United States. This involves the certification of aircraft, pilots, maintenance technicians, maintenance and training facilities, and virtually everything pertaining to aviation that requires approval. In addition to the above, the FAA operates the airspace system, provides for aviation security, and engages in engineering and development aspects associated with planning the new airspace system. All of this adds up to an awesome responsibility and requires the efforts of several thousand persons. The largest of the FAA's duties is to maintain the air traffic control system.

The air traffic control (ATC) system consists of three related facilities within which the air traffic controller works.

1. *Flight Service Stations* provide pilots with weather, emergency services, advisories, and flight planning assistance. There are some seventy-five such stations within the United States and its territories. There were once two hundred more FSSs, as they are known, but because they are becoming automated, positions were gradually phased out.
2. *Air Route Traffic Control Centers* control aircraft flight between airports and maintain safe separation of aircraft. There are twenty-one centers presently operating. Each center has responsibility for about one hundred thousand square miles of airspace.
3. *Airport Control Towers* handle approach and departure aircraft as well as those that are moving on the ground at the airport facility. There are approximately 272 airports with

FAA control towers and 224 more under contract operators for a total of 496. So, about half are operated by
FAA controllers, while the others are contracted to private
companies.

The FAA employs more than fifty thousand people. The diversity of jobs within the FAA rivals that found within the airlines.
The FAA hires controllers, maintenance specialists, pilots, financial planners, engineers, analysts, managers, technical writers, public relations personnel, human resource staff, and many other kinds
of workers. Let's look at a few of the major areas of employment.

Air Traffic Control

The air traffic control (ATC) specialist controls aircraft and maintains safe separation of aircraft in the air and on the ground. The
three types of facilities mentioned above dictate to a great degree
what the controller does, although the basic training is the same.
The successful controller talks with pilots, makes use of radar, has
an excellent understanding of weather phenomena, recalls numbers
well, and is able to communicate fluently.

About fifteen thousand air traffic controllers work at FAA ter-
minals and other facilities in the United States. The controller's
union, the National Air Traffic Controllers Association, known as
NATCA, estimates that one thousand additional controllers are
needed to meet existing system requirements. Of the controllers
currently working, about half will retire between now and 2010.
The mandatory retirement age is fifty-six. Each year 5 to 8 percent of the workforce retires, or otherwise leaves the profession.
That will continue each year between 2003 and 2007.

Education

The applicant for ATC must have three years of work experience that demonstrates potential for learning and performing air traffic control work. Formal education may substitute for work experience. An excellent score on the aptitude examination, or having certain aviation certificates such as a private pilot or instrument rating, will also substitute for work experience. The ATC system is drawing significantly greater numbers of college graduates than in previous years. Major changes have taken place in the way applicants are screened for ATC training. Past screening took eleven weeks at the FAA's academy in Oklahoma City. The failure rate was often as high as 60 percent. That screen has now been reduced to one week. It has not been determined as yet whether one is better than the other for selecting controllers. It is better in that one does not remain for several weeks and then possibly fail the screen. It also saves the government considerable money in housing, food allowance, and instructor salaries.

Working Conditions

A controller works inside year-round. The tower controller rotates from a dark room filled with radar scopes to the "cab" of the tower, where the controller handles aircraft by sight and radio contact. The tower is preferred by some because of the variation in jobs performed during the day.

The air route center controller spends the workday, or night, inside a building without outside reference. The work shift is spent talking with pilots, while watching the representation of the pilot's aircraft on a radar screen. The only variation is working different sectors of airspace. Some controllers who rise to training and supervisory levels may spend time training other controllers.

The flight service controller has the greatest variety of activity. He or she assists pilots in preflight briefings, talks with pilots over the radio and telephone, assists in emergencies, helps lost pilots find a safe airport, and generally acts as a public relations person for safer flight. The controller in all of the facilities must be quite adept at operating a computer terminal.

Salary

The ATC specialist will earn a salary that is second only to the captain with a major airline. Upon completion of the schooling at the ATC Academy, the controller will normally begin work at a government service salary schedule level of GS-7. This figure is currently $27,185 per year. As the controller progresses toward the full performance level (FPL), salary increases will come about every six months. Within five years, and upon reaching the FPL, the controller should be at a base salary in the vicinity of $60,000. The top end base salary of a GS-14/step 10 controller is $88,096. The rate of pay for the controller in the en-route center is higher than in the flight service stations (FSS) and most towers. The tower option is divided into five levels based upon the amount of activity at the tower. Level five affords the highest pay rate. Level five towers are those found at airports like Atlanta, Chicago, Los Angeles, and Dallas-Fort Worth. The controller receives premium pay (additional pay) for shift work, weekends, and holidays, which can substantially increase earnings as much as 40 percent.

Employment Outlook

In 1981, President Ronald Reagan fired eleven thousand air traffic controllers who had gone on strike in violation of federal law. For a number of years the need for controllers was tremendous. University cooperative education programs expanded. New hires were trained by the hundreds. Prior military controllers were recruited. During an FAA freeze on hiring that went into effect in 1993, few controllers were hired. The FAA later estimated that it would probably need some five hundred new controllers per year. Actual hiring depends on budget authorizations.

The FAA once operated many level-one towers, mostly at small Visual Flight Rules (VFR) general aviation airports. However, it now contracts that out to private companies. These are additional places for persons interested in ATC to ply their trade. Civilian training is available. However, one needs to be careful where such training takes place; not all facilities are equal.

The Bottom Line

ATC affords an excellent opportunity for a satisfying career with superb financial reward. It takes a particular kind of person to pass the rigorous screening and training required. However, you are assured of a special place in life if you qualify. A person must not have reached the thirty-first birthday in order to be considered for the tower and en-route center positions. The FSS controller may be older. Rapid increases in base salary occur with additional training and proficiency. A person can hardly be closer to aviation than by being an air traffic controller.

FAA Operations and Maintenance Inspection

There are several positions within the FAA that are associated with performing inspections. The requirements and the duties are quite varied, yet fall into basically four major categories:

1. *Operations inspectors* are pilots who perform duties primarily associated with evaluating other pilots.
2. *Maintenance inspectors* are those who perform inspections of technicians and facilities where maintenance is performed.
3. *Avionics inspectors* are inspectors who evaluate avionics technicians and their workplaces.
4. *Manufacturing inspectors* are those who work with the companies that develop and build airline and general aviation aircraft.

• *Operations inspectors.* These FAA employees operate in two spheres of activity. One group works with air carrier operations and the other group within the general aviation system.

The air carrier inspector has responsibility for scheduled air carriers, supplemental carriers, air travel clubs, and commercial operators that fly aircraft weighing more than 12,500 pounds. The general aviation inspector has responsibility for examining pilots and flight instructors and evaluating pilot training schools. Both types of inspectors investigate accidents. Both must be highly qualified pilots. Females account for about 2 percent of all air carrier safety inspectors.

• *Maintenance inspectors.* The duties of these inspectors involve evaluating maintenance technicians, repair facilities, maintenance programs of training schools, and maintenance programs of either general aviation operators or air carrier operators. These inspectors are normally separated in the same manner as the operations inspectors, working either with air carriers or with general aviation operators.

• *Avionics inspectors.* These inspectors evaluate avionics technicians and repair facilities, inspect aircraft for compliance with regulations, and investigate and report on accidents, incidents, and violations. They specialize in either general aviation or air carrier–type operations. The inspectors must have three years of avionics supervisory experience on the type of aircraft to be inspected.

• *Manufacturing inspectors.* These inspectors have the responsibility of administering and enforcing safety regulations and standards for the production of aircraft. The FAA inspector is included by the manufacturer early in the plans for new aircraft and continues to monitor the project throughout the manufacturing and testing of the airplane, until the airplane receives FAA certification. This is a costly process for the manufacturer and one in which it is important that the FAA be involved from the beginning.

This inspector must have a background in quality control methods and in the manufacturing of aircraft, engines, or components. The inspector must be able to evaluate whether the aircraft meets design specifications and airworthiness standards before a certificate may be authorized. He or she may also be involved in approving modified, import, military surplus, and home-built aircraft. Females make up about 17 percent of aviation manufacturing safety inspectors.

The inspectors in all of the aforementioned categories may work out of district FAA offices or manufacturing inspection district offices. Some may work in Oklahoma City at the National Field Office of Aviation Standards. There are approximately 108 flight standards district offices and 4 manufacturing inspection district offices throughout the United States, along with about 30 other inspection and certification facilities.

The inspector's knowledge and experience are the foundation upon which our system of air safety regulation depends. Inspectors will continue to receive recurrent training throughout their careers.

Salary

FAA inspectors are normally hired at a GS level between 9 and 11, although some, because of extensive experience and certification, may be hired at as high as a GS-15. GS-9 is presently $33,254. GS-11 is $40,236. There are ten steps within the government service pay scale for each GS level. A GS-11 could earn $52,305 at step ten. The current maximum basic pay for GS-15 under the government pay scale is $103,623. GS scales go up yearly. Additional pay is given for shift work, holidays, and weekends. The FAA points out that locality pay can often add thousands of dollars a year to the GS base pay, depending on where in the country you work.

Employment Outlook

The position of inspector is not a position that one can rely on being available with consistency. Some years are good hire years, others are not. Since inspectors normally come from other aviation careers into the FAA, it makes good sense to retain the aviation job you have and wait to make application for the position of inspector until the announcement of hiring occurs.

The Bottom Line

The job of an FAA safety inspector is never routine. Almost every day is different from the previous day. Depending upon which category of inspector one may be, he or she is likely to visit a training school one day, conduct a line check of pilots at an air show the following day, inspect the facilities of a major carrier another day, and ride in the jump seat of a 747–400 to review the crew coordination. Of course, there is always plenty of paperwork. One inspector indicated that a person would have about two days of paperwork for each day in the field. An inspector must be able to communicate well, both verbally and in writing.

The pay is very good. The working conditions are usually superb, except perhaps when investigating an accident. Recurrent training keeps the inspector on the cutting edge of technological change. The operations inspector, for example, may go to school several times per year to maintain currency on different aircraft, such as a corporate jet, a jet helicopter, or a turboprop twin.

Engineering and Testing

The FAA must have the services of engineers and those who work with engineers. The FAA needs almost every type of engineer, but particularly the aeronautical, electrical, electronic, mechanical, and civil engineer. The engineer works on research and development problems associated with aviation, such as aircraft noise, instrument landing systems, airport construction, and especially those elements that will enhance flight safety in the air or on the ground.

Education

The engineer will have graduated from an accredited engineering college or university. The engineer may already have gained valuable work experience prior to joining the FAA. Most engineering schools provide cooperative education opportunities for their students. This allows the engineer to gain excellent work skills while attending college.

The engineering aide and engineering technician assist the FAA engineer by drafting plans, conducting necessary tests under the guidance of the engineer, setting up laboratory equipment, and assisting in preparing technical reports. The technician is normally senior to the aide and will be hired at a higher GS pay level. The duties required of the technician normally involve more responsibility than do those of the aide.

The technician and the aide may receive their formal education within a college, a technical institute, or a private proprietary school. The engineering technician may be certified by the Institute for Certification of Engineering Technicians (ICET). Graduation from a school recognized by ICET will normally ensure greater acceptance of a technician within the industry.

Working Conditions

Most work is conducted inside within a laboratory or outside supervising or observing tests on aircraft and components. Some travel is necessary in order to gather information, observe tests at other facilities, or consult with airport administrators about local problems. Engineers and their assistants may work at FAA headquarters in Washington, D.C.; at the FAA Technical Center in Atlantic City, New Jersey; at NASA sites throughout the United States; at certain military bases; or at one of the eight regional FAA offices.

Salary

Engineers may be hired at a level as low as GS-5, which would be very unusual, and as high as GS-14, depending upon past experience and educational background. It would be common that one be hired closer to the GS-14 than the GS-5. The GS-14 in step one earns around $67,765 per year. This would be for a normal forty-hour week. Additional compensation is earned for unusual working conditions.

Technicians and aides may be hired at levels from GS-1 up to GS-12, with the technician being employed at the higher level. They also work a forty-hour week. Some travel may be required, but not as frequently as for the engineer. Federal jobs allow a liberal travel allowance for trips required of an employee's particular position.

Employment Outlook

The FAA, like many other government and nongovernment organizations, hires engineers on a rather consistent basis. The employment of technicians and aides usually is much less consistent. You must keep in contact with the FAA district office to learn of announcements for aides and technicians. Employment with the FAA, as with many other government entities, requires considerable patience on the part of the applicant. It is not unusual for the process to take from nine months to a year—even when they want you.

The Bottom Line

Working in engineering with the FAA can be exciting and very rewarding. You are compensated well, are constantly on the frontier of change in aviation, and usually work in pleasing surroundings. If you have a particular penchant for design, modification, or innovation, this may be just the place for an interesting aviation career.

Civil Aviation Security

The FAA utilizes persons in two types of work related to security. They are either special agents or federal air marshals (FAMs). The principal work of the security agent is to inspect airports in the United States and in foreign countries where air carriers from the United States fly. They ensure that the airports are safe and that operational plans related to explosives, weapons, a sterile gate area, and hazardous materials are effective. Some agents may conduct drug investigations and background checks on applicants, as well as investigation into FAA employee misconduct.

The FAM does the same things as the security agent when she or he is not working as a FAM. As a FAM, the individual will fly on selected high-risk airline routes to deter hijacking and to ensure the safety of passengers and crew. In order to be a FAM, one must successfully complete an eleven-week course of demanding physical and mental training at Quantico, Virginia. Training includes qualification with a pistol, which requires a score higher than that required of secret service agents; specialized law enforcement training; and intensive practice in team work.

Education

A college degree is required and graduate study is required for appointment at or above the GS-7 level. Experience may substitute for some education or education for experience. The hiring procedure may be hastened for one having a grade point average (GPA) of 3.5 on a 4.0 scale, a demanding requirement by anyone's yardstick. Those who do not qualify with a high GPA must take the Administrative Careers With America (ACWA) examination given by the Office of Personnel Management (OPM).

General experience requirements give some insight into the type of education desired in order to develop the necessary skills. You should have experience that will assure that you can understand legal provisions, regulations, and administrative procedures and be able to apply them. You also must have the ability to analyze written and numerical data, draw conclusions, and make decisions. The ability to communicate effectively, orally and in writing, is obviously required, as it would be of nearly any position in today's workplace.

Working Conditions

The federal air marshal and security agent travels approximately 60 percent of the time on the job. The FAA normally assigns most employees to a specific region, and about 75 percent of the travel will be to facilities within that region. The remaining 25 percent may be throughout the world as needed. The marshal and agent can be sent to any country to which a U.S. airline travels. That includes nearly all of the world's countries.

Much of what the marshal does is considered classified information and is not available to the general public. Most of the job will be concerned with whether airports and airlines are complying with FAA regulations regarding baggage, individuals, transportation of hazardous materials, and general security measures. Additional work involves investigations of in-flight incidents of hijacking, bomb threats or explosives, illegal activities, and improper conduct in or around FAA facilities.

The agent is involved in reviewing a great amount of paperwork that is required to comply with federal aviation regulations. The marshal also travels aboard designated flights to review the security measures involved and spends a considerable amount of time in trying to "crack" the security involved in boarding a plane without proper clearance. The marshal may also try to pass through airport security while carrying a weapon, such as a gun or an illegal knife, to test the effectiveness of the security system. This is probably some of the more fun activity of the marshal, although not something to be taken lightly.

Training of the federal air marshal is also part of the working conditions, because much time is spent in training. The marshal undergoes a basic training program of eleven weeks in Quantico, Virginia. The agent and marshal engage in four two-week training sessions at the FAA Academy in Oklahoma City. Three hours of physical training are required each week throughout the marshal's career.

The marshal must also engage in weapons firing each month. You can see that this is a most demanding job. The marshal also submits to random drug testing on a frequent basis. The marshal must take a complete physical examination each year, similar in nature to the Class II Airman's Medical Certificate. If older than forty years of age, the marshal will undergo an annual electrocardiogram (EKG) to determine heart condition.

Salary

Specialized experience of the applicant will determine the entering salary. One year of such experience allows the federal air marshal to enter at the GS-7 grade, two years at the GS-9, and three years at the GS-11 or GS-12 level. The job announcement outlines the various experiences that qualify as specialized experience. Experience as a compliance inspector, investigator, analyst, planner, auditor, or investigative journalist may qualify. Experience in legal work or specific knowledge of the laws and regulations in assessing compliance are areas that are considered important.

The new federal air marshal is normally brought into the security division as a GS-7. Salary range in 2002 was $31,500 to just over $80,000. A team leader can earn up to $98,000 a year. Salary differs with overtime, supplements for being away from home, other government service credits, and a host of other situations that affect rates of pay.

Employment Outlook

The FAA has established a federal register for marshals and agents in much the same manner as for other FAA positions. Announcements may be obtained from the Office of Personnel Management or from local offices of the FAA. Position on the register is determined by your test score and whether you have a veteran's preference (ten points are added to the score of the qualifying veteran). The number of marshals and agents hired will vary each year. A region of the FAA may hire as many as thirty new marshals or agents in a given year, while other regions may hire none.

The Bottom Line

The civil aviation security agent's job is one of great importance to the nation. More than 450 million people fly within the United States each year. The agent protects these people from external threat by ensuring that airports and airlines engage in an active security program of compliance with federal regulations. The present job outlook varies considerably from year to year. The pay is satisfactory the first few years and becomes quite good from about year four on. The job involves travel and is exciting for a person who likes to travel.

However, the job announcement is quite clear that the marshal or agent, especially when in the field, may be subject to high risk of personal injury, either in self-defense or in defense of others. This is not a warning to take lightly. Other field work, while perhaps not dangerous, is physically demanding. The amount of time spent away from home also may be disruptive to family life. But if you want to travel extensively, would like to carry a firearm, appreciate physically demanding work, can communicate well, and enjoy interacting with others, being a marshal or agent may be for you.

Security measures tightened in 2002 in reaction to terrorist attacks on the United States, and the FAA and the new Transportation Security Administration added more security positions. There is a greater need now for well-trained security personnel than ever before.

Transportation Security Administration (TSA)

The new focus on security means more jobs. Airport security has already been tightened, airliners have been redesigned, and more such changes are yet to come. It is not yet clear how many permanent new jobs there will be for security personnel. There will be more ground level jobs, such as security screeners, as well as airborne jobs in the expanded federal air marshals program.

Some thirty thousand screeners will be needed in airports, according to U.S. Secretary of Transportation Norman Mineta. These were brought under federal jurisdiction, as part of the newly formed Transportation Security Administration under the Department of Transportation.

Screeners will check passengers at all airports. Job candidates will have to pass an aptitude test for federal civil aviation screeners and a background check. They are required to be U.S. citizens with a high school diploma. They'll undergo special training by the TSA, designed to improve airport security to new levels, before they start their jobs. Pay will be improved from earlier screener salary ranges to attract more and better candidates. Salaries will range from $23,000 to $40,000.

More federal air marshals are being trained and deployed by the FAA civil aviation security office at this point. Additional marshals will be needed, even after the current crisis is over, as air traffic grows in the coming decades. The majority of candidates will come from criminal justice backgrounds, although the FAA also considers aviation management degrees desirable as a job credential. Multiple hires will be made to staff bases at major metropolitan airports around the country. They have to be eligible for a top-secret security clearance.

Many airports are reviewing their security plans and appointing security directors, so there should be new management-level jobs emerging here, too. The jobs are not easy, but they are vital and those who qualify will probably be well compensated.

Other FAA Positions

The FAA hires numerous individuals who do not have education or experience directly related to aviation. The FAA employs physicians who study the effects of flying on the human body, who help establish standards for the three classes of FAA medical examination, and who conduct research into stress related to careers such as air traffic control.

The FAA utilizes lawyers who represent the FAA in legal matters, who help write FAA regulations, and who assist in developing agreements with foreign airlines.

The FAA also hires urban planners, airport safety specialists, economists, mathematicians, budget analysts, property and material managers, accountants, and others. Of course, a large organization must have a variety of workers such as secretaries, librarians, typists, mail clerks, computer programmers and operators, and those with an assortment of skills. Whatever your aspiration is in terms of a career, the FAA may be an excellent place for you to apply those skills you learn.

In addition to working for the federal government, one can find excellent positions with state governments and with associations at the national level.

State Aeronautics Agencies

Each state has an aeronautics office, commission, agency, or some form of state regulatory unit that, among other functions, is the conduit for state funds to airports and aviation-related functions within the state. The state unit may be as small as one person or as large as several dozen employees. In addition to approving grants to airports for construction, maintenance, and runway improvement, some aeronautics offices are responsible for flying the governor, the cabinet, and other state dignitaries. Some states fund workshops for teachers, where they can learn about the benefits of aviation and pass the information on to their students. Some states offer youth camps, in cooperation with Scouts or the Civil Air Patrol, where young people can learn about aviation careers, the history of aviation, and rocketry. The young person may begin flying, gliding, or ballooning at such camps.

If the aeronautics office is one of the state's larger units, it will have several divisions. One division may focus on engineering and help to plan and develop airports and airport expansion. Another division may hire professional pilots and maintenance technicians who fly and maintain a fleet of airplanes for the state. Yet another division may consist of employees who work with air pollution and noise abatement procedures at the major carrier airports. Each office will have an administrative division, which handles the reams of paperwork associated with millions of aviation user-tax dollars that are dedicated to improving the aviation infrastructure. In most states, the office uses funds collected exclusively from taxes paid on airline tickets and aviation fuel sold. Thus, such services in no way take away from highways, schools, or the social welfare system.

Because of the unique nature of each state aeronautics office, it is not possible to describe all of the potential career opportunities available. Each state is organized in a different manner. Some aeronautics offices are autonomous. Some are under the state department of transportation. In some states, the state's air national guard transports the governor and state officials. You will need to check with your state to determine what career opportunities exist.

The kinds of positions for which you may prepare yourself in order to work for a state aeronautics agency are: pilot, maintenance and avionics technician, civil engineer, draftsperson, administrator, aerospace educator, environmental engineer, and accountant, to list a few.

It is always helpful to develop good communication skills, regardless of the position you choose to hold. At some point in your career, you may speak before groups or have to defend your operational budget or present your ideas to committees for approval. Once you feel comfortable speaking before peers, you will be much more effective in defending ideas before supervisors or the boss.

Nearly three thousand people are employed by state aeronautics offices. A National Association of State Aviation Officials (NASAO) survey of states in 1995 indicated that if the federal government began to allow aeronautics offices to administer federal airport grant funds, the states would need an additional 169 employees, mostly grant managers and compliance officers, within one year of such authorization.

National Association of State Aviation Officials

The National Association of State Aviation Officials (NASAO) is the organization that represents and lobbies for the various state aeronautics offices. Several professional positions exist in NASAO, involving research, public relations, and dealing with the U.S. Congress, with airports, and others. In recent years, NASAO has offered an internship program in its Washington, D.C., headquarters, which really is a full-time paid position for a specific period of time, usually one year. This provides an excellent opportunity for the newly graduated aviation management major.

States provide a regulatory function for aviation organizations that operate only within the state. The FAA obviously regulates aviation within the United States. NASAO assists in preventing conflicting legislation between state and federal agencies, as well as promoting uniformity among the laws and regulations of the various states.

As you seek a career in aerospace, look at state and federal organizations and governments. They offer outstanding opportunities for learning, for a career of service, and for a stimulating way of life.

7

AEROSPACE INDUSTRIES

THE AEROSPACE MANUFACTURING industry in the United States consists of approximately eighty major firms. These companies are engaged in designing, developing, manufacturing, and selling airframes, engines, avionics, and components. All of these items are necessary to fly and maintain the thousands of different aerospace vehicles used around the world.

One of the major contributions of the aerospace industry is that it provides a favorable balance of payments between the United States and other countries. That is, the United States sells more aerospace products to other nations than it imports. In the mid-1990s, the export value was $40 billion, with 80 percent of that in civil products, mostly large passenger jets. The United States has traditionally purchased more than 60 percent of the aerospace goods produced by U.S. manufacturers. The coming wave in aerospace manufacturing is toward consolidation and international alliances. This may have some effect on personnel needs of manufacturers.

Since manufacturing is so broad and requires such a diversity of talent and skill, it is impossible to list all of the positions available. Thus, this chapter will be concerned more with describing the major divisions of the industry, where the production facilities are located, some specific jobs for which you may qualify, and what the outlook is for the twenty-first century.

Manufacturing of Major-Carrier Aircraft

For years the three manufacturers of large civil transport aircraft in the United States were, in order of production, Boeing, McDonnell Douglas, and Lockheed. Lockheed has stopped producing commercial air carriers and concentrates on military aircraft missiles and space-oriented products. With virtually no competition, the big three dominated world air transport production. Then a European consortium began developing Airbus Industries. It was not long until Airbus surpassed McDonnell Douglas in selling its several models of the Airbus 300. It rivals Boeing today and could rise to first place in the near future. However, Boeing and McDonnell merged in 1997, in part to become more competitive in a global marketplace. Large civil air transports are not the sole production of these huge manufacturers. Most are heavily involved in military aircraft, helicopters, military weapon systems, spacecraft, and other products as well as civilian aviation.

Boeing

The Boeing Aircraft Company in Chicago dominated the market for large airliners almost from its inception. At one point it controlled over 65 percent of the world's market. That has slipped some, but Boeing is still very strong. It is estimated that the world's air carriers, including those that build smaller regional airliners, will purchase more than eighteen thousand aircraft between now and 2020. That will be worth in the neighborhood of a trillion dollars. Many are projected to be of the large air carrier variety. This ensures that Boeing will remain strong.

Boeing's main plants are located in Auburn, Everett, and Seattle, Washington. It also has facilities in Portland, Oregon. The mainstays of Boeing's production continue to be the 737, now the most popular short-to-medium haul aircraft; the 757; the 767; and the huge 747. The 777, newest in Boeing's line, joins this awesome group. The production of 747s, still the world's largest civil air transport, is close to fifteen hundred units, many of which have been purchased by Pacific Rim nations such as Korea, Japan, Singapore, and Hong Kong. Boeing has production facilities in several parts of the United States and some foreign countries. However, if you want to work on large airline airframes with Boeing, as of now, you'll have to go to Washington.

McDonnell Douglas was very successful with the short-route model DC-9, which has now been through several modifications, all selling well throughout the world market. The Super-80, followed by the DC-9 and now the MD-90 and 95, are serving this part of civil aviation. These models are particularly popular with the "hub-and-spoke" concept of air travel. This concept utilizes a central airport into which smaller aircraft fly and redistribute passengers going to other cities. Some carriers use several hub airports. Among the more well-known airports and airlines using them are United Airlines in Denver and Chicago, American Airlines in Dallas and Chicago, and Delta in Atlanta and Dallas.

McDonnell Douglas was the nation's number-one defense contractor. Its merger with Boeing created an aerospace colossus. It generated some $900 million in free cash in 1994, indicating how strong its position was in the manufacturing world. One of its strengths lay in its military helicopter program. McDonnell Douglas was headquartered in St. Louis, Missouri. Somewhat like Boeing, it has plants in various locations. Its last independently designed major aircraft, the MD-11, was manufactured up until 2001, and the large fleet of existing MD-series jets is still maintained by Boeing, along with engines and parts. It was principally the replacement for the DC-10, a workhorse of a medium- to long-range route aircraft. Douglas had streamlined its production so that it could break even by selling around sixteen aircraft annually, whereas it takes most companies some forty units to recoup their initial investment.

The combined company is at work on a new "sonic cruiser" aircraft that can maintain speeds just under Mach one—the supersonic threshold—for extended high-altitude flights.

Boeing now has a strong mix of military and civil aviation products. This affords extra diversity in a post-cold-war world moving away from military production. If you are seeking a company with the widest of manufacturing interests, both civil and military, this may be your company.

Lockheed Martin

Lockheed Martin Corp., headquartered in Burbank, California, is an old name in large airliners as well as military production. The last commercial success in air carrier aircraft for Lockheed was its L-1011 Tristan. This was a medium- to long-range aircraft capable of carrying from 250 to 400 passengers, depending upon the model. The L-1011 was known as "the pilot's airplane" because pilots loved to fly it. Lockheed sells some civil versions of its popular military C-130 to third-world countries that have need of such an aircraft to operate into unimproved airfields. The joint strike fighter project is one of the largest aviation developments now under way anywhere in the world. Lockheed is the lead partner.

General Aviation Manufacturing

During the late 1970s, the general aviation (GA) industry was building and selling more than seventeen thousand units per year. The bottom dropped out of the market in the early 1980s, and by 1986 fewer than fifteen hundred units were being produced annually. Interestingly, while total production dropped by 90 percent, the dollar figure of aircraft produced dropped only 50 percent. Those aircraft remaining in production were the more expensive turboprops and executive turbojets.

Aircraft during the 1980s were increasing in price by quantum leaps, due in large part to product liability costs associated with the American tendency to take the manufacturers to court with every accident. What is ironic is that while there was such an inclination for court battles, the GA industry was experiencing a 50 percent decline in accidents. Corporate aviation accident rates are the lowest in the nation and rival the safety figures of air carriers. In 1993 there were *no* U.S. scheduled airline passenger fatalities. Experts at Aerospace Industries Association, Washington, D.C., predict an overall world market for 3,200 new civil aircraft (including some 375 commercial airliners worth $25 billion) valued at $34 billion in 2002. About 800 to 900 business jets a year are being sold.

The major U.S. manufacturers of GA aircraft are Cessna, Learjet, Beech, Gulfstream, and Piper. There are other manufacturers, but their production does not compare to the big five.

Building aircraft is a labor-intensive industry. It requires great skill learned through years of apprenticeship and practice. Overall, the drop in production during the 1980s devastated the industry. Cessna alone went from more than twenty thousand workers to fewer than five thousand. Not only does this affect those who lose jobs, but also it affects the future of the industry when there are fewer opportunities for young people to learn the necessary skills. It also has its effect when the industry recovers and wishes to rebuild itself.

Cessna

Cessna was the world's leader in single-engine piston aircraft during the years of producing training and personal aircraft of two and four places. When that market ceased, Cessna became the leading producer of executive jets. The Cessna Citation model leads the field today because of price, ease of operation, and its ability to get into smaller airports. It is a good "step-up" aircraft from the twin turboprop. Every two years when the Special Olympics are held, corporations fly competitors into the Olympic site. It is something to see nearly three hundred Citations flying into one city.

Cessna indicated that it would resume production of its 172, 182, and 206 models after Congress enacted product liability laws.

President Clinton signed such a bill late in 1994, called a Statute of Repose, and Cessna intends to produce two thousand units per year. This provides a much-needed boost to the industry. Cessna selected Independence, Kansas, as the site of the new factory. About one thousand employees work there. The 172 Skyhawk model, its best selling aircraft, is now sold around the world.

Learjet

Bombardier of Canada owns the Learjet Company. This is a further indication of the consolidation and international nature of the aerospace industry. Several Lear models are produced. The Lear is a very popular aircraft for advanced training and for military use, and it is the second leading executive jet in terms of numbers produced. William Lear conceived and built the first executive jet for the corporate market. He also invented the car stereo. The production portion of the company is headquartered in Wichita, Kansas.

Beech

The Beech Aircraft Corporation, now owned by the Raytheon Corporation, Lexington, Massachusetts, is the leading producer of turboprop executive aircraft and of a regional airliner, the Beech 1900. The 1900 is so popular that Beech cannot keep up with its demand. It claims 70 percent of the nineteen-seat regional airline market. Beech bought the patents for the Mitsubishi Diamond, a turbojet executive aircraft, and now produces the Beechjet. It also produces several personal-type airplanes and the very different Starship, an executive aircraft with pusher props, a leading edge canard, and a glass cockpit. However, the Beech King Air is still the bread and butter aircraft.

Gulfstream

Gulfstream Aerospace Corp., a General Dynamics company, builds the top-of-the-line executive aircraft. The G-V is its premier executive aircraft today, priced at over $30 million. By 2001 more than 160 G-Vs had been sold. It holds records for speed and distance in its class. New mid-size jets, the Gulfstream 100 and 200, fly intercontinental routes for businesses and carriers such as China's Hainan Airlines. The G-IV and G-V are also used extensively by the air force, which flies the president, vice president, and other VIPs on trips that do not require the Boeing 747. Gulfstream is located in Savannah, Georgia.

Piper

All of the GA manufacturers dropped training aircraft from their inventory for a period of time. Piper hit hard times and tried a comeback with training aircraft late in the 1980s. The company emerged from a reorganization effort as the New Piper Aircraft, Inc. Piper still does quite well in producing high-end piston singles, such as Meridian, and piston twins, like the Seminole. In fact, Piper earned $181 million in revenues in 2001 on sales of 440 aircraft. Piper is located in Vero Beach, Florida.

Employment with Other Manufacturers of Aircraft

We have discussed primarily the development and building of the major-carrier airplane and the top manufacturers of corporate and training aircraft. By doing so, we risk leaving out some other important firms that have been developing excellent airplanes for decades.

Just one example: Dassault Aviation, a European company that makes the Falcon jets, has production facilities and sales offices in the United States, as well. You may find great opportunities with a company like this and other specialty aerospace firms. However, the production of such airplanes is somewhat like the automobile production of Ferrari or Lamborghini: very few are built each year by skilled craftspeople to fill custom orders. Our interest is to provide information that will give you the best opportunity for employment, and so the focus has been with the larger companies that hire the most people.

Education

Aircraft manufacturers seek the most highly qualified and educated person they can attract, just as in all other areas of aerospace. Everyone likes to hire experienced and skilled craft workers. However, companies are realistic and understand that their needs are often greater than the supply of such workers. A high school diploma normally is required, unless you have a skill or trade that is of particular value to the manufacturer. College or technical school training is recommended.

Manufacturers hire a great number of professionals each year. Aeronautical and industrial engineers, computer specialists, supervisory personnel, aircraft safety specialists, and numerous other workers in various job categories make up some of the hiring needs. Administrative positions—usually requiring a college degree—have such titles as contracts administrator, materials manager, compliance director, and production manager.

Certification

We have said previously that the aerospace industry is one of the most regulated industries in existence. Since the FAA has the certification responsibility for all U.S.-manufactured aircraft, it stands to reason that manufacturers like to hire workers who are also FAA certified. In fact, aircraft manufacturers compete with the FAA, the airlines, and general aviation for certified maintenance and avionics technicians. The aircraft industry has need for people trained or experienced in metal work. The person who can form, weld, size, or inspect metal forming can expect a welcome reception by the aircraft industry.

Composite materials are becoming popular in constructing airplanes of all types. Many of the major-carrier aircraft have some composite surfaces. Some general aviation aircraft are built exclusively from composite materials, although these tend to be found more in the home-built category. Preparing yourself to work with composite materials may ensure you have a place in this industry.

Working Conditions

Manufacturing of almost any description can be quite demanding, both physically and psychologically. Employees often work near large machines, loud riveting guns, and cranes that may be constantly moving large items overhead. Huge assembly plants may not have ideal climatic conditions, being either too hot or too cold for comfort. Many of the plants hire thousands of workers and operate several shifts. This may mean walking a great distance from a parking place into the plant, working a night shift, and interacting with all kinds of people. Unionized plants have their advantages and disadvantages: an established grievance process, usually higher pay, but also the cost of dues and the possibility of strikes, with the attendant loss of several weeks of pay if contract negotiations are terminated.

Try to choose an employer and a plant where the work ethic is valued and all workers do their share of the work. There have been reports of workers who were asked to falsify information related to work on government contracts.

You can perceive these conditions as negative and find the manufacturing workplace a hostile environment in which to earn a living. On the other hand, you might find a challenge in such circumstances and could enjoy bringing creativity and innovation to the job site. There are many positive aspects to working in the manufacturing industry. The pay is usually adequate, the benefits superb, and the opportunity for continued employment fair. There have been large employment swings in this industry, depending upon the national economy, the defense buildup, and the extent to which the potential purchaser has accepted new technology. However, if you are skilled in a particularly needed area, long-term layoffs will not likely affect you.

Salary

Rates of pay will vary depending upon whether one is skilled, certified, or experienced as well as whether one is salaried or classified—salaried being those in administration and classified usually being those who are blue-collar or hourly workers. Additional factors affecting pay will be the economic condition of the company, the geographical region of the nation in which the company is located, and, to some degree, whether the company is unionized. There are nonunion companies in which pay and benefits exceed those of unionized plants, but this is still somewhat rare.

Some examples of current pay rates for a large aircraft manufacturer in the Southeast will give you an idea of how the industry compensates its employees. Table 7.1 represents beginning hourly

Table 7.1 Rates of Pay for Company X, Southeast United States

Job Classification	Beginning Hourly Rate
Utility person	$10.40
Metal sizing	$13.00
Shop dispatcher	$14.00
Form operator	$15.00
Inspector	$15.50
Electrician	$15.50

rates for each classification, as of the late 1990s. Pay increases are given every six months. At the end of three years, the utility person will be earning $14.25 per hour. If the utility person is attending school or learning a trade, it is possible that he or she could change classification and move to a different labor grade.

Professional employees normally are on a fixed salary, which may change, depending upon how the supervisor rates the employee or perhaps what kind of profit margin the company had the previous year. Beginning salaries for professional employees can vary by several thousand dollars per year. A college graduate may begin as an entry-level professional for around $22,000 per year with one company. Another company across town may employ a graduate with a degree in technology as a space-packaging engineer for $31,000. Companies associated with military and space manufacturing will call almost everyone an engineer, whether or not they actually have an engineering degree. It looks better on paper. The technologist may be performing the duties formerly accomplished by an engineer. There is a tendency for companies to hire engineers for positions that do not require an engineer. Some forward-looking companies are realizing that college graduates with technology degrees often can perform tasks once thought to be the province of engineers only. The technology graduate will likely be more satisfied than an engineer, who may feel underemployed while performing routine tasks.

The college graduate who is qualified to work for an aircraft manufacturer will likely have a starting salary in the mid- to upper $20,000 level. The engineer will probably begin in the low- to middle $30,000s. Mid-management personnel will earn between $55,000 and $72,000, and executive directors will earn about $80,000.

Employment Outlook

Nearly everyone is happy that most of the world's major military powers are at peace. However, this state of affairs has impacted manufacturing companies that depend heavily on military contracts. Decreased demand, severe production overcapacity, and the recession have combined to affect aerospace manufacturing employment negatively for some time. However, in 2002 the federal defense budget increased dramatically. Hiring will occur selectively and in certain regions more so than others. Some specialties will continue to be strong, but it is difficult to predict the future demand in other sectors. If you want to avoid layoffs, develop skills that are transferable to either sector—civil or military aviation.

The U.S. aerospace industry employed 791,000 people in 2000; of these, about 223,000 were engine and aircraft production workers. The industry goes in cycles. Ironically, in terms of profit, 1994 was a banner year at $5.2 billion for aerospace manufacturers, although that year saw a decline in the total workforce. There is optimism that an increase in civil aircraft manufacturing, forecast at 2 percent a year, coupled with a strong space program, may offset some of the losses. Although the climate in congressional leadership favors the space program, it competes heavily with funding areas where there is more demand by the public.

Those working within the aerospace manufacturing industry felt some impact from a business downturn in 2000–01. Aerospace, however, is an industry that will remain as a major force in the U.S. and global economies. Perhaps as you decide upon a career you should give thought to developing skills and expertise that are usable within the broad fields of manufacturing.

The Bottom Line

The manufacturing industry is gigantic. It generates billions of dollars, employs hundreds of thousands of people, and is a net exporter credited with helping the nation maintain a better balance of trade with other nations. The industry employs workers to provide all types of skills, trades, expertise, and professional services. There are both positive and negative sides to working within the industry. On the one hand, the pay can be good. You may choose to live in a variety of states and still work in this industry. The work itself can be exciting and challenging. On the other hand, this field is subject to fluctuations in employment, due primarily to the economic health of the nation and the state of foreign affairs. Some people might find the workplace uncomfortable and the work itself tedious. Your own feelings about these aspects of manufacturing will determine whether it is a good field for you.

Aircraft Engine Manufacturers

Early developers of flying machines often had to build their own engines because either what they needed was not available, or general engine manufacturers did not want their names associated with those "crazy flying people." The major problem of existing engines in the early days of flight was their size and weight. The engines were massive and extremely heavy. We are fortunate that engines have progressed right along with airframes, giving us more powerful engines than normally needed to do the job. The United States is also a major manufacturing center for jet and reciprocating engines. Engine developers are divided by the market for which they produce, just as are the airframe manufacturers.

Air Carrier Engines

There are basically three manufacturers of engines for the major-carrier aircraft. One is General Electric (GE) of Lynn, Massachusetts. GE is supplying a large number of engines for the 747 series as well as some smaller models. Like several of the airframe companies, GE has plants in various locations. The company's main competitor is Rolls-Royce of England. Rolls-Royce's purchase of Allison Engine Company for $525 million gives Rolls a seamless and complementary range of engines from those used in small corporate jets to the one-hundred-thousand-pound thrust of the Trent 800, which will be one of the three engines used on the Boeing 777. The Trent is the first of these engines to attain certification. Some of the large buyers of major-carrier aircraft can specify which engine they prefer when they order their jets. Pratt-Whitney in Hartford, Connecticut, a United Technologies company, and its Canadian branch have also come on strong in recent years in building large jet engines for fighter aircraft and commercial jets. These companies compete for business.

General Aviation Engines

Practically all small-engine manufacturers produce smaller jet and reciprocating engines. In addition to the firms already mentioned, general aviation suppliers include Textron Lycoming of

Williamsport, Pennsylvania; Teledyne Continental of Mobile, Alabama; and Pratt-Whitney. Continental and Lycoming are the principal manufacturers of piston engines for the small training aircraft.

Education and Employment Outlook

If you want to work for an engine manufacturer, you should have a good background in engine mechanics. Some of the same skills found in airframe manufacturing are needed. One element of continued production by engine makers is that an engine usually wears out well before the airframe does. This requires either new engines or remanufactured ones. Larger conglomerates have bought the majority of smaller engine manufacturers, and this tends to give greater stability to workers. The outlook for engine manufacturing of both air carrier and general aviation engines appears quite solid.

Military and Space Manufacturing

Many of the major manufacturers of air carrier aircraft and engines also are involved in developing and building defense and space vehicles. There are several companies that concentrate almost exclusively on the latter. A few of the companies are General Dynamics, LTV Corporation, Lockheed Martin, Rockwell, Thiokol, TRW, and Grumman-Northrop. The acquisition of Vought Aircraft and Grumman Aircraft by Northrup foreshadowed the consolidation that is taking place in the industry. In 2002 Grumman-Northrop offered to buy TRW as well, indicating that the consolidation trend continues.

Lockheed merged with the Martin-Marietta Corporation to create the world's largest defense manufacturing company. This consolidation positioned both companies, already independently strong, to be a major force in selling missiles, fighters, spacecraft, and other components. Together these companies employ some 130,000 people. The merged companies earned sales revenues of more than $25 billion in 2000. Lockheed Martin was the number-one defense contractor in 2001. Its biggest job was to produce twenty-two joint strike fighters for use by the U.S. armed forces, a $19 billion project.

One of the problems associated with the military industrial base is that the United States has been sliding in high technology leadership for several years. At the same time, foreign countries have been increasing their abilities in military and space vehicles and weapons. Only the strong, multicompany conglomerates may continue to successfully exist. Such companies often hire—and subsequently lay off—thousands of workers at a time, depending upon government contracts. The current peace initiatives of much of the world may further depress the military side of the manufacturing industry. Space exploration, civil transport, and other innovative means of transportation may take up only a portion of the slack from a military employment downturn.

Space limitations in this book do not permit us to fully explore the military and space manufacturing industry. There are many similarities between this portion of the industry and what has been described in the aircraft and engine manufacturing sections. The major difference is the user of the product. The U.S. government buys the majority of military and space components, but that has fallen from 56 percent to 40 percent since 1987. Such products also are sold to many foreign nations with which the United States maintains good relations. The United States presently is cooperating with other nations in building military products for joint use. Japan, the European Space Community, and Canada cooperate on space development. The future of space exploration may well be a collective effort, and collective manufacturing will occur with greater frequency. Right now, in 2002, missiles and space vehicles employ about twenty-one thousand U.S. production workers and about eighty-seven thousand people in all U.S. enterprises.

Russia has become the major cooperating nation with the United States in the space effort. The projected space station will be largely U.S./Russian built and occupied. The Space Shuttle docked with the MIR space station that Russia maintained as the longest-lived space vehicle in history. A Russian cosmonaut was on board the shuttle in the fly-by early in 1995. Combined international crews now operate the new International Space Station, the largest spacecraft ever built. The first crew came aboard in June 1999: International Space Station Commander Bill Shepherd, astronaut; Soyuz Commander Yuri Gidzenko, cosmonaut; and Flight Engineer Sergei Krikalev, cosmonaut.

For many portions of the military industry, a security clearance is required. This involves a thorough investigation of your past activities, associations, and loyalty to the United States. Such clearances range from the lowest level—confidential—up to top secret, depending upon the nature of the project. A word to the wise: security clearance requires a personal record free of any drug violations, a criminal record, or other problems.

8

MILITARY AEROSPACE

THE MILITARY PROVIDES excellent career opportunities for the aviation or space enthusiast. Practically every skill needed in civilian aviation is also needed by the various branches of the military. Every branch trains pilots, controls airports, maintains planes, has some involvement in the space program of the nation, and has a part in the manufacturing process of military aircraft, missiles, spacecraft, and weapon systems.

The military not only offers aviation careers, but is an excellent training ground for future civilian aerospace careers. Many civilians who are air traffic controllers, airline pilots, airport managers, and maintenance personnel received their training in the military. The Federal Aviation Administration (FAA) has a process whereby military experience can substitute for civilian experience in obtaining pilot and maintenance certification, depending upon the level of experience achieved.

The added advantage of aerospace training in the military is that you may remain in an active reserve unit upon separating from the military. This allows you to maintain military skills, receive pay and benefits while serving, develop your civilian career, and ultimately receive excellent retirement benefits from the military. You enjoy the best of both worlds.

Each branch of the military substantially trains its own aerospace workers and professionals. Some people view this as unnecessary and a duplication of expense. Others suggest that each branch has a different aerospace mission, hence the need for separate training. There are several similarities among the various branches. These similarities—such as salary, benefits, and employment outlook—will be considered toward the end of this chapter.

United States Air Force

The United States Air Force (USAF) has the largest contingent of bases dedicated to aerospace. The training of air force pilots consists primarily of preparation for bombing, fighter engagement, air transport, satellite deployment, air-to-air refueling, reconnaissance, and transportation of the President of the United States, as well as top civilian cabinet members and members of Congress, on fact-finding missions. The air force had approximately 385,000 active duty personnel in the year 2000. Nonfemale minorities account for 21 percent of active duty forces. Females make up about 19 percent of active duty personnel.

Education

A college degree is required to become a pilot. The preferred degree is engineering. However, the air force has accepted pilot candidates with practically every college major known. The ultimate education for a career would be graduation from the Air Force Academy in

Colorado Springs, but only the finest candidates need apply. The academy receives about twenty thousand applications yearly, for an entering class of around thirteen hundred. In addition to high test scores, a superb high school record, and some athletic ability, the candidate must have a congressional or presidential appointment. Other routes to commissioned officer status and a pilot slot are through Air Force Reserve Officers Training Corps (ROTC), offered at numerous colleges and universities around the nation. You may also apply to attend officer candidate school.

Female pilots may currently fly any aircraft including combat aircraft. The North Atlantic Treaty Organization (NATO), of which the United States is a member, was the first to allow female combat-aircraft qualified pilots. Several of the instructors in both basic and advanced jet trainers are women. Lt. Colonel Eileen Collins was the first female pilot to fly the Space Shuttle. She did so in January of 1995. All-female crews are approved for operating missile silos, and all-female crews have routinely flown the large four-engine C-141 jet cargo airplane. The air force has approximately fifteen hundred women pilots.

Positions in aerospace for commissioned officers literally fill pages and pages. The education required for such entry will depend upon the position to which you aspire. A discussion with the local recruiter will get you started toward your career.

Other aerospace jobs that do not require being a commissioned officer will require a high school diploma. The air force will further the training of recruits going into such positions.

Working Conditions

The air force officer and enlisted person work throughout the world, depending upon the career specialty chosen. Even within those countries where there are no military bases, American military personnel are assigned to U.S. embassies.

The range of working conditions in the USAF would fill a book. You may be stationed in a missile silo in Iowa, working several hundred feet below the earth's surface, or be in the test center in Ohio perfecting the latest flight simulator. Assignment may take place with the joint military space effort at Colorado Springs or may involve advanced wind-tunnel testing in Tennessee. An operational unit in Spain or Japan may require your expertise. You may have some choice of assignment, depending upon your training and the needs of the USAF.

Actual working conditions for USAF personnel are normally pleasurable—in peacetime. Many jobs are not much different from comparable civilian jobs. Of course, the military does operate around-the-clock, 365 days a year, so you will receive some night, weekend, and holiday duty. In times of meeting deadlines, you may very well work twenty-four hours a day. During an emergency or armed conflict, you can throw the clock out the window!

The USAF wants you to continue learning. You may attend selective technical schools, command schools, or leadership schools for upper-level enlisted persons. Certain programs will allow you to complete college as an enlisted person, after which you may qualify for officer training. Such working conditions can be quite desirable.

United States Navy

The United States Navy has many of the same aerospace missions as the air force. However, many of those missions will be conducted from aircraft carriers and submarines instead of large air bases located on land. The navy does have several land bases for flight training, for long-duration overhaul and maintenance, and for technical and command schools. The Marine Corps, during times of armed conflict or war, becomes a part of the navy. However, the marines are represented by equal command on the Joint Chiefs of Staff, who advise the President on defense matters.

The navy has around four hundred thousand active duty personnel. Minorities account for about 26 percent of active duty forces, and females make up approximately 14 percent of active duty personnel.

Education

Naval officers must be college graduates. The navy has an excellent program of education, beginning with the U.S. Naval Academy located in Annapolis, Maryland. The naval academy is much like those of the air force and army. The graduate receives a bachelor's degree, frequently majoring in engineering, and may take a commission as a navy ensign or Marine Corps second lieutenant. Approximately 1,350 candidates are accepted yearly. The navy also provides education aboard ship in many areas of the world. Enlisted personnel normally have a high school diploma, and many have experienced some level of postsecondary schooling. The educational level of those in all service branches is increasing.

Working Conditions

The navy enjoys a varied existence on the water, beneath the seas, and in the air. Ships that support aircraft carriers and submarines that carry missiles can be as large as a small city. Thousands of people may serve aboard a carrier. Several hundred will carry on duties aboard a sub-tender. There are machine shops on board that allow skilled workers to manufacture almost any part needed to sustain the operations of both branches.

The navy has nearly six hundred ships and almost six thousand aircraft. The nearly one-million-strong force includes active duty and reserve officers, enlisted personnel, and civilian employees. Working conditions vary according to the assignment. Submarine crew members can be underwater for up to seventy days at a time, longer for special research programs similar to those conducted under the ice at the north pole. Aircraft carriers can be deployed for more than six months and longer in times of armed conflict. Conditions can be cramped and unpleasant aboard ship, especially for enlisted persons. The workday can be exceedingly long when a carrier is constantly deploying aircraft. The exposure to wind, sea, and sun can be uncomfortable at times. The navy requires a special kind of person, one who thrives on accomplishment, challenge, stimulation, and commitment.

United States Marine Corps

The United States Marine Corps is an independent service but exists within the Department of the Navy for administrative purposes. We will look at the Marine Corps briefly in order to distinguish between some of the programs, assignments, and different aircraft flown. The marine is normally stationed at bases that include both navy and marine personnel. Marines are stationed aboard ship, at U.S. embassies, and at major bases like those at Quantico, Virginia, or Parris Island, South Carolina. The Marine Corps has one particular motto that is rather apparent, regardless of the skill or job function. Marines say that the person is a marine first, and a pilot second—or whatever specialty for which the marine is trained. And a marine may have to grab a gun and hit the ditch in an emergency! The Marine Corps has about 174,000 active and reserve personnel. Twenty-seven percent are nonfemale minorities. Females account for around 6 percent of active duty forces.

Education

The official marine policy is "stay in school." You must be a college graduate to be commissioned. If you are a graduate of the naval academy, you may choose either the navy or the marines. Some navy ROTC programs at selected colleges also allow you to choose the marines. A popular program for receiving a Marine Corps commission is the platoon leader's class (PLC). A freshman or sophomore can spend two six-week terms at the officer candidate school in Quantico, Virginia. A junior attends one ten-week session. Upon graduation from college, the person then receives a commission. There are two added educational options available. You may postpone active duty if you are pursuing a law degree or if you are in an aviation pilot's option. Further information on these programs is available from recruiters. Depending upon the needs of the corps, a limited number of guaranteed flight positions are given to university students, normally at the freshman or junior levels. The marines fly some 980 aircraft, of which 528 are rotorcraft and 452 are fixed wing. Included in the inventory are the F-18 Hornet, Harrier II, EA-6B's Sea Knight, Super Stallion, Huey, and Cobra.

Seniors, and those having already graduated from college, may elect to attend an officer candidate class, which affords the same opportunities as for those engaged in PLC training. Superior high school students may qualify for a navy ROTC scholarship. This will provide four years of tuition, books, fees, and about $100 per month for up to forty months. Your military training will take place during the summers, with a six-week cruise aboard ship following your freshman year, four weeks of warfare specialties training following the sophomore year, and a precommission training period between the junior and senior year.

Women may qualify for a commission in the Marine Corps, but there are differences in the periods of training and scholarships that are available. Most of the continuing education programs available to the navy officer or enlisted person are available to the marine.

Working Conditions

The Marine Corps has the reputation of needing "a few good men"—and women—but it is equally known for having the toughest training of any of the service branches, except perhaps for advanced training as a navy seal or army ranger. The marine is the first to hit the beach during wartime. The marines are usually the ones sent in to "hot spots" like the Middle East. The training required to produce such soldiers has to be hard. Not everyone can qualify to be a marine.

The other side of the coin is the opportunity to see the world and to serve in visible places like the White House, American embassies, aboard the marine helicopters that carry the President, or aboard ship traveling to distant ports.

The marine aviator flies types of aircraft not flown by any other U.S. service branch. Marines fly the Harrier, which is a vertical take-off fighter. It is capable of supersonic speeds and has the ability to maneuver like a helicopter. The marine pilot also flies the free world's largest helicopter. The Marine Corps is looking for an aircraft that can take off and land like a helicopter, but can then rotate its engines and fly like a fixed-wing turboprop. This machine would have commercial uses if the marines can perfect it. So if you like unique aircraft, you may qualify to be a marine and fly such innovative machines.

United States Army

It may surprise you to learn that the U.S. Army has the largest fleet of aircraft of all the military branches. The total inventory of active aircraft in 1995 for army reserve, National Guard, and active army units was 7,164. Of these aircraft, 94 percent were helicopters, used primarily as troop support gun platforms and for transporting air cavalry troops to the front line. The army also has a full complement of fixed-wing airplanes, used primarily to transport senior officers and to act as fire direction control for artillery and air force fighters. These army pilots are called forward air controllers (FACs). A large number of aircraft are set aside for training new pilots to replace retiring personnel and those who leave the service for jobs as civilian pilots. Contracted civilian flight instructors accomplished much of army flight training, leaving the army officer free to fly with line units.

Females make up around 15 percent of active duty army personnel, but so far, only about 3 percent of the 12,500 pilots. However, the first U.S. females to be trained in combat aircraft are in the army. They fly the Apache, Cobra, or Kiowa helicopters. The United States Army has some 530,000 active duty forces. Of active duty personnel, nonfemale minorities account for 36 percent.

Education

The army seeks to recruit high school and college graduates and is the largest single employer of American youth. Many of the officers come from college or university ROTC units. A full ROTC scholarship, given to exceptional high school graduates, can amount to $20,000 or more per year, depending upon the college or university chosen by the student. The ultimate career opportunity exists for graduates of the U.S. Military Academy at West Point, New York. Many of the most famous American generals and military tacticians have been West Point graduates. Entrance to the academy is highly competitive, as are the navy and air force academies. Congressional appointment is required but does not ensure acceptance.

The army, like the navy and Marine Corps, has a special rank related to aviation that is somewhat in between senior enlisted and commissioned officer status. It is called "warrant officer" and is something of a holdover from early flight during armed conflict, when all branches allowed enlisted pilots. The warrant officer is assigned primarily to helicopter flight. In fact, the school that supplies many of the helicopter pilots also provides that when the enlisted person completes the course, he or she is designated a warrant officer. This rank commands most of the respect and military courtesy of the commissioned officer. Some warrant officers may command a unit, although it does not happen often. Command normally goes to commissioned officers. Warrant officers usually are required to complete at least two years of college to remain on active duty. Continuing education opportunities abound at most army bases, allowing one to complete a degree or a skills program that also has applicability to the civilian market.

Working Conditions

The aerospace worker in the army may be assigned to a major over-haul facility or training command such as Fort Rucker, Alabama, or to operating units like the 101st Airborne at Fort Campbell, Kentucky. Assignment to foreign posts such as South Korea or West Germany is common. Many of those associated with army aviation will spend a considerable amount of time in the field, honing military skills and learning how to stay operational in the face of adversity. As with every aviation unit, there will be a need for pilots, maintenance and avionics technicians, loadmasters, gunners, air traffic controllers, and other specialties.

The soldier has thirty days of leave (vacation), rather good pay and benefits, respect from civilian employers when the service period is completed, and the opportunity to see some of the world. Long hours, assignment to dangerous or unpleasant places, and the strict discipline of military service isn't for everyone. However, within the army, aviation is one branch that is particularly exciting and one that can prepare you for an aerospace position in civilian life.

United States Coast Guard

The United States Coast Guard is a branch of the Department of Transportation during peacetime. During war, the guard becomes a part of the U.S. Navy. The Coast Guard performs some of the same functions as the navy. In particular, it fights drug smuggling, rescues people stranded at sea, and protects U.S. ports and ships. The Coast Guard is actually older than the U.S. Navy is.

Education

The Coast Guard accepts persons between the ages of seventeen and twenty-six. The U.S. Coast Guard Academy, like other service academies, accepts high school graduates between the ages of seventeen and twenty-two. It is located in New London, Connecticut. Approximately 275 cadets are selected annually from five thousand applicants. Unlike the other service academies, there are no congressional appointments or quotas. Acceptance is strictly on merit. People who possess a bachelor's degree and are between the ages of seventeen and twenty-six may take a seventeen-week officer candidate course (OCS) and become a commissioned Coast Guard officer. Outstanding enlisted personnel may be commissioned through OCS as well, but must complete a bachelor's degree before promotion to Lieutenant Commander. Other people who are licensed merchant marines, graduates of a maritime academy, former military pilots, or lawyers may become Coast Guard officers through other programs. Women have the same opportunity for selection as men. They serve in all classifications. Although the women's Coast Guard was a separate entity during World War II, it is fully integrated today.

Working Conditions

The Coast Guard officer or enlisted person performs many duties similar to navy personnel. During wartime, the Coast Guard escorts merchant ships through unfriendly waters and may patrol foreign coasts to prevent enemy shipping. During the present peacetime, the Coast Guard is heavily involved in slowing down drug traffic into the United States. Such work can be dangerous. The Coast Guard also establishes regulations for building oil tankers. The Coast Guard performs an education function for boaters, teaching them the rules of safe boating. The Coast Guard auxiliary patrols offshore to rescue stranded boats. Much of this work is performed by volunteers who fly their own aircraft in particular search patterns before sundown.

Aviation plays a major role in the Coast Guard. Airplanes of many descriptions are involved in search and rescue, long-range patrol, and iceberg location. Everything from helicopters, which can land in the water or on land, to the mammoth, four-engine Lockheed Hercules transport plane are used by the Coast Guard. The guard operates 130 helicopters and 73 fixed wing aircraft. Their inventory includes 236 ships of 11 different varieties.

The Coast Guard can be an exciting way of life, but the working conditions can be equally hazardous. You must be prepared to work long hours during major emergencies and during search-and-rescue operations. However, the pay and benefits are equal to other service branches, the educational and retirement benefits are good, and opportunities are available for travel to exotic places. The combination of ships and aircraft may be what you seek.

The Coast Guard is not a large branch, as compared to other branches of the service. There are about thirty-six thousand active duty personnel and an additional eight thousand reserve members. Some six thousand civilian personnel are utilized, just as with other service branches. About thirty-five thousand auxiliarists serve as volunteers. If you have an interest in the service, either as a uniformed member or as a civilian worker, you should contact the recruiter near you. Replacements for retiring and departing personnel are always in demand.

Military Salaries and Benefits

Salaries and benefits are generally the same for all branches of the armed forces. The government periodically alters pay grades. Retired members of the service receive a cost-of-living increase, which retirees of most nongovernment jobs will not receive. This alone can be of considerable importance when planning for a comfortable retirement.

Current salary levels for enlisted persons range from $12,000 per year for the new recruit to $36,000 for the top grade. Additional compensation may be allowed for separate quarters, subsistence allowance, incentive pay, special allowances, hazardous pay, and flight pay. Many of these allowances are tax-free, which can measurably add to the money you keep. Certain of these allowances are for married enlisted personnel only.

Officers receive $24,000 per year starting out as a new second lieutenant and can get up to $79,500 as a colonel with twenty years of service. Pilots receive additional incentive pay in the neighborhood of $125 per month to $650 per month, depending upon the number of years of service as an aviation officer. The amount of time spent in service—referred to as "longevity"—will make a difference in salary, in addition to the rank one holds. Officers receive many of the additional benefits given to enlisted personnel, plus a uniform allowance.

Some of the military services have a problem with retaining pilots who have met their obligation. Higher pay from the airlines draws many pilots to the civilian market. Attempts to stem this tide have taken several forms. Bonus programs of up to $12,000 per year for re-enlisting have been offered for air force pilots and are sometimes offered for the other services. Allowing pilots to fly longer, instead of being forced into administrative positions, also seems to have been important in retaining pilots. Bills have been introduced by Congress to raise pilot salaries and require longer periods of service for those trained as pilots in the future. Many military pilots leave active duty for an airline career. Others remain and retire from the military at twenty years and are still eligible for around fifteen years of service with the airlines. The potential career earnings in a combined military/airline career can amount to around $4.5 million. This figure includes all salary and retirement benefits.

Additional perks for military personnel come in the form of possibly teaching at one of the service academies, or perhaps flying or working on one of the world-famous aerial demonstration teams like the Thunderbirds or Blue Angels. The army also has the Golden Knight Parachute Team, which provides exposure similar to top entertainers in the civilian market. Many of the military bases field competitive sports teams, especially in those sports associated with the Olympics.

Travel to great places all over the world can be a part of military service. If the foreign bases allow dependents, the service will pay for household goods and automobiles to be shipped to the duty station. When quarters are not available on base, housing allowances provide for the family to live in the foreign communities. This can be a tremendous adventure for a family. Foreign dependent schools normally are available for the children of service personnel. Special educational programs often are available for the service person as well as family members. Officers are particularly encouraged to continue their education through graduate degrees.

The Bottom Line

Military service can be an excellent way to receive training for future civilian work or a wonderful place to have a career. If you enter the service at a young age, you can retire before the age of forty and still have many productive civilian years left for another career. You can enter a reserve or National Guard unit and build points toward a career. The reserve or National Guard officer or enlisted person can qualify for many service schools and thereby develop the abilities to rise in rank and experience. The author knows of one person who served only two years of active duty time, except for schools; who went through pilot school, medical officer's school, special forces, and airborne training; and who is now a three-star general! Only your own initiative and abilities limit you. Consider the military as an excellent opportunity for advancement.

National Oceanic and Atmospheric Administration

The National Oceanic and Atmospheric Administration (NOAA) is the smallest of the uniformed services. It is listed only because it offers some aviation flight and maintenance opportunities. The officer with NOAA goes through an officer candidate program similar to that for officers of other services. The officer candidate must hold a bachelor's degree in science or engineering and meet the physical requirements. Women are accepted for any of NOAA's officer positions. Women have been on NOAA ships since 1972, involved in both diving and flying.

The newly commissioned NOAA officer must serve a tour on ship before qualifying for training as a pilot. Most assignments are for two to three years. Diver training is somewhat more available than flight opportunities. You definitely do not want to combine diving with flying! In fact, if you become a pilot and then decide to become a diver, even for fun, maintain strict discipline about avoiding flight immediately after diving. You can end up with decompression sickness, or "the bends," and wake up with a sheet over your face!

NOAA has twenty-three ships at sea. They operate from Nor-folk, Virginia; Seattle, Washington; and other ports around the world. Officer training takes place twice a year at Fort Eustis, Virginia. Each session lasts fifteen weeks. Application may be made to NOAA, 11400 Rockville Pike, Rockville, Maryland, 20852. Advanced graduate work is recommended and is provided for the officer wishing to pursue such study.

9

NATIONAL AERONAUTICS AND SPACE ADMINISTRATION (NASA)

AERONAUTICS AND ASTRONAUTICS are terms that describe careers or occupations as well as the science of flight and space flight. The National Aeronautics and Space Administration, or NASA, is involved in developing and testing flight vehicles that operate in both environments. NASA also is responsible for studying the benefits of aeronautical and space activities and for cooperating with other nations in space and aeronautical pursuits while still preserving the role of the United States as a leader in aeronautical and space accomplishments.

Congress created NASA in 1958, a year after the Soviet Union launched the world's first satellite, Sputnik, into orbit around the earth. Prior to this event, the airspace of sovereign nations was considered inviolable—that is, not to be trespassed upon. Sputnik violated this principle every ninety minutes as it circled the globe. Many nations around the world were outraged. The United States was particularly upset, as it had been the world's technological leader for more than a century and suddenly saw its biggest enemy paving the way into space. Americans seethed with resentment and embarrassment and resolved to catch up and surpass what the Soviets had accomplished. The American education system was seen as the means to accomplish this goal. The United States simply had to educate more and better scientists, engineers, and mathematicians. Those of you who seek positions in the fields of aeronautics and astronautics are the beneficiaries of this determination, born out of cold war hostility, yet still thriving in today's era of global cooperation led by the United States and the former Soviet Union. We seem light-years away from the cold war years.

NASA's Occupation Classification System

NASA classifies work based upon what tasks workers perform, not upon what their educational background may be. Of course, your educational background dictates to a great degree what kind of work you are capable of accomplishing.

NASA has ten major classifications or subgroups of its aerospace technology system. The life sciences division is further divided, but we will look at only the basic ten divisions:

1. space sciences
2. life sciences
3. fluid and flight mechanics
4. materials and structures
5. propulsion systems
6. flight systems
7. measurement and instrumentation

8. data systems
9. experimental facilities, equipment, and operations
10. administration and management

Space Sciences

This area of investigation is concerned with planetary research as well as observation of distant stars, other galaxies, extraterrestrial phenomena, and solar terrestrial research. NASA scientists are interested not only in what is happening in space, or how planets and galaxies may have been formed, but also how such knowledge may relate to improving life on earth. Many of our present orbiting satellites give data on weather, crops, infestations, forest fires, and other elements of our environment, which will assist us in using and preserving that precious environment.

Interest Areas

You may enjoy a career within NASA's space sciences division if you are interested in the principles of meteorology or astronomy or in the technological application of scientific inquiry. College majors in astronomy, astrophysics, geology, geophysics, mathematics, meteorology, and physics are most closely associated with such careers. NASA sites where you are more likely to be employed in space sciences are the Ames Research Center, Goddard Space Flight Center, Marshall Space Flight Center, and the Stennis Space Center. Addresses of these facilities are listed at the end of this chapter.

Life Sciences

Investigation in the life sciences is concerned with two principal areas. The first is the study of the effects of exposing biological organisms to space. The organism may be a human, a monkey, bees, or any form of life on earth that can be a part of a mission into space. Some study is conducted on earth to simulate the space environment.

The second aspect of the life sciences involves understanding the origin of life on earth. Several programs are included in researching this aspect of science. The life sciences workers help design life-support systems for astronauts, explore adaptive behavior of plants and organisms, design closed ecosystems for extended space travel, develop tools for humans working in space, and deal with numerous other aspects of life and travel beyond our earth.

Interest Areas

The life sciences divisions of NASA hires people with background and education in anatomy, chemistry, botany, biology, physiology, geology, and other life sciences. If your interest is in the origin of life or in extraterrestrial travel, the life sciences divisions of NASA may hold interesting work for you. Employment in life sciences will more likely occur at Ames and Johnson space centers.

Fluid and Flight Mechanics

NASA is never satisfied with state-of-the-art flight mechanics. NASA is always working on the future, whether it is in aerodynamic vehicles, rocket or jet engines, or general aviation training aircraft. Motion mechanics forms a significant part of the research conducted. Automated controls and how pilots react to certain flight displays are important to the future air traffic system. NASA applies what it learns during in-flight experiments conducted in NASA aircraft.

Interest Areas

Particular areas of expertise utilized by this division include engineering physics, astronautics, mechanical engineering, physics, and other physical sciences. Mathematics is acceptable if coupled with a minor in a physical science. Employment in fluid and flight mechanics occurs at all NASA locations except Stennis and NASA headquarters.

Materials and Structures

This division is concerned with designing spacecraft materials and forming such materials into shapes that will withstand the tremendous forces of supersonic and space flight. Operation in space presents special problems that most of us never consider. How do we lubricate a space shuttle; can we use the same grease found at the local service station? Do the temperatures of space affect the spacecraft, thus requiring special insulation materials? If we use very heavy and very thick metals, how do we compensate for the added weight we must thrust into space? These are only a few of the questions considered by scientists and workers in this division of NASA.

Interest Areas

College graduates and others with special knowledge in ceramics, physics, metallurgy, chemistry, and various branches of engineering are important to this division of NASA. NASA employs materials and structures specialists at all sites except Stennis and NASA headquarters.

Propulsion Systems

The single item that probably limited the possibility of flight until 1903 was the lack of an engine that was both lightweight yet powerful enough to lift the aircraft off the ground. The same limitation exists for the future of flight. The projected space plane, which would transport the commercial passenger from New York to Tokyo in less than three hours, will combine both known and presently unknown principles of propulsion. Flight to other galaxies will require propulsion systems capable of much greater speeds than we can currently produce. These are a few of the propulsion problems NASA will try to solve.

Interest Areas

The specialist in propulsion must know about fuel-and-air mixing; heat transfer; energy conversion devices; solar, chemical, and nuclear sources of energy; and how such systems will react to space travel. A background in chemistry, physics, engineering, astronautics, or other physical science, along with an excellent foundation in mathematics, will assist you in obtaining employment with this division of NASA. Employment in propulsion systems is found more frequently at Goddard, Johnson, Kennedy, Lewis, and Marshall centers.

Flight Systems

We immediately think of a flight system as either an airplane or a propulsion system coupled with an airfoil. This is partially true, but not comprehensive enough. A flight system may be a probe, an orbiter, a payload, a launch vehicle, or even a test facility. An operational flight system is a combination of mission, payload, vehicle, instrumentation, and experimental design. There is also a lot of "what if" deliberation surrounding the operation of a flight system.

Interest Areas

People with expertise in engineering, physics, mathematics, and especially computer science are necessary to the development of flight systems for NASA. Flight systems staffers work in all NASA centers except Stennis and NASA headquarters.

Measurement and Instrumentation

When NASA deploys a mission, several hundred workers sit in front of panels of instruments, as well as computers, and monitor what is happening to the launched vehicle. The myriad dials, flashing lights, meters, and scales give specific data to the people skilled in monitoring the instruments. Telemetry is received on the propulsion systems, the spacecraft itself, the astronauts, and the environment surrounding the craft. All aspects of the launch program, mission, and recovery depend upon the specialists who monitor the instruments. These specialists also design and test new instruments under all kinds of conditions, including simulation. An example of such instrumentation is a tiny radio transmitter designed to be swallowed by an astronaut to give core body temperatures during a space mission.

Interest Areas

Areas of study for people seeking positions in measurement and instrumentation include electronics, physics, mechanical engineering, and computer science. Measurement and instrumentation specialists are employed in all centers except Stennis and NASA headquarters.

Data Systems

The ability to enter space, perform work, and return safely depends upon many specialties, not the least of which is computer science. The exploration of space probably could not exist without the computer technology that grew as a result of space exploration. One depends upon the other. The supercomputers—such as the Cray series—advance the opportunities of space exploration. Literally dozens of specialties have grown within the computer field, in large part because of the space program's needs. The technology transfer to the everyday world of work was so rapid that many people not only have a computer on their desk at work, but also one at home. Some even carry a small laptop aboard airliners.

Prior to the computer sophistication of today, the development of aeronautical vehicles often took years of trial and error, hugely expensive tests in wind tunnels, and the risk of lives of pilots as they flight-tested the vehicles. Today, the vehicle can be drawn, tested, modified, and the flight test simulated on the computer. This saves millions of dollars and untold amounts of time. The vehicle must still be built and flight-tested, of course, but at that point many of the questions have already been answered.

Interest Areas

If you enjoy working with computers and asking "what if" questions, then you may enjoy working in data systems. A combination of computer science, mathematics, and some area of physical or biological science is recommended for entering this futuristic field. Data systems employs persons at all NASA sites except Stennis and NASA headquarters.

Experimental Facilities, Equipment, and Operations

Engineers and technicians must have equipment to work with and an environment within which to work. This is the task of people who work within this division of NASA. They plan, design, and construct wind tunnels, cryogenic laboratories, solar collection systems, aircraft crash test facilities, and laboratories for investigating liquids and gases used in research programs. This brief list only scratches the surface of equipment and facilities needed in today's research environment.

Interest Areas

Workers in this division come from aeronautical engineering, architecture, ceramics, electronics, metallurgy, and a host of other engineering disciplines. The facilities division hires workers in all locations except Stennis and NASA headquarters.

Administration and Management

The last word in NASA is administration. Any organization, especially one the size of NASA, must have an extensive web of management and administrative support. NASA installations are spread worldwide. Persons of every employment description work for NASA. The efforts of hundreds of workers must come together flawlessly during a major mission, and countless hours of coordination and interaction must precede a NASA mission or major experiment. All of this comes together only with the proper management and administrative support.

Interest Areas

Managers tend to rise from within an organization, although some special skills may be brought in from outside. Highly skilled workers of the nature of NASA employees usually prefer that managers also be highly skilled in one of the disciplines they will supervise. This makes the manager "legitimate" in the eyes of the workers.

If you wish to rise into management, you should be prepared in one of the scientific disciplines and should add courses in the behavioral sciences. Management personnel are located at all NASA sites. Those located at NASA headquarters are normally senior-level personnel, not entry-level.

Technical Support Positions

All of the aforementioned classifications of NASA careers utilize a large number of professional personnel. However, these professionals need the support of an extensive array of technical, clerical, and crafts personnel. Many of these positions will require high school and some postsecondary technical education. Many community colleges, technical institutes, and private proprietary schools provide the training required to work with NASA or with a NASA contractor.

NASA has its own apprentice program for a variety of needed skills. A good high school record and an abiding interest in the technical area are prerequisites for entry into such an apprentice program. These positions are very competitive. It will serve you well to be involved during high school in science fairs, clubs, and summer programs of a scientific nature. It will not hurt to live close to one of the major NASA sites that have apprentice programs. These sites are listed at the end of this chapter.

NASA utilizes workers in electronics, optical fabrication, machine operation, metallographics, pattern making, and numerous other skilled trades. Some of these may be entered through the apprentice program, for which you must take the Civil Service Examination to qualify. NASA has prepared a number of free career-oriented materials to share with you. Just write to one of the locations listed at the end of the chapter with your request. You might specify which areas interest you most.

Since NASA employs many engineers and scientists, you may obtain a feel for the type of salaries paid by reviewing Chapter 4 on engineering research and development. Technicians earn much less than those who have graduated from college, but even their salaries are normally higher than those of the average American worker.

NASA and NASA contractors need clerical workers, analysts, computer programmers, receptionists, file clerks, mail clerks, and executive secretaries. Whatever your line of interest or skill, there may be a position for you in the nation's space program.

NASA Astronaut Selection and Training

Most of you reading this book will not remember a time when there were no astronauts. For the author and many of his contemporaries, flying into space once was a thing only for comic book characters, the Saturday serial at the local movie theater, and science-fiction nerds in the chemistry club. How far we have come!

Today, NASA routinely recruits pilots and mission specialists who hurtle into space at speeds in excess of twenty thousand miles per hour. It does take a special breed of person to do this. It also takes special skills and knowledge, which can be learned in school. Do you have what it takes to make it into space?

Astronaut Selection

The first American astronauts were selected in 1959. There were seven of them. Of the ones still living, one retired as a navy admiral, one became a senator, and several became corporation presidents. All are popular speakers at conventions and group meetings.

Three years after the first selection process, the selection of Gemini and Apollo astronaut trainees began. Six of the original seven had flown in the Mercury project. The second group followed much the same career path to becoming astronauts as the original group. They were skilled in flying high-performance jet aircraft. They graduated from college with an engineering degree and were in excellent physical condition. The maximum age had been decreased from forty to thirty-five and the maximum height limit increased from five feet eleven inches to six feet.

The third selection took place in 1963 and began changes that are still in place today. NASA was seeking outstanding academic qualifications. The four hundred applicants had a doctorate or equivalent experience in the natural sciences, medicine, or engineering. Similar selection processes have taken place on an announced basis since this time.

Astronauts are selected from two groups today. There are pilot candidates and mission specialist candidates. The pilot candidate must have a bachelor's degree in engineering, a biological or physical science, or mathematics. He or she must have at least one thousand hours of pilot-in-command flight time in high-performance jets. Flight-test experience is highly desirable. The pilot candidate must pass NASA's rigorous Class I physical. More specific information is available directly from NASA.

The mission specialist must have a bachelor's degree in the same areas as specified for the pilot. The candidate must have three years of related experience in the field. A graduate degree is preferred and may substitute for some experience. The candidate must pass a NASA Class II physical. An astronaut candidate from Canada recently joined twenty other candidates for a year of training.

Astronaut Training

The astronaut candidate remains a candidate for only a year. During that time, the astronaut candidate is evaluated on the ability to perform under zero-gravity conditions. This is accomplished while suited in a bulky space suit within the neutral buoyancy tank or aboard the modified KC-135 called the "vomit comet." The candidate also is evaluated in the laboratory and with fellow candidates. Teamwork is a must in space. Everyone's life is dependent upon every member of the team.

If the candidate survives the year of evaluation, he or she then is elevated to astronaut status. This is when the training really begins. Pilot astronauts will continue to fly aircraft that simulate characteristics of the space shuttle. They also will fly many hours of missions in the shuttle simulator, honing skills of docking, maneuvering, and reacting to simulated emergencies. The mission specialist will continue to study in the primary discipline, design space laboratory experiments, interact with contractors on payloads, attend engineering conferences, and advise other astronauts of what is taking place within their areas of responsibility. All astronauts must maintain top physical condition.

Astronauts are assigned to specific flights by means known only to NASA. Some astronauts may wait years to be assigned to a mission. Others may fly fairly soon after selection. Payloads are assigned to specific missions in relationship to what is to be accomplished. Mission specialist astronauts will conduct experiments related to their discipline, insofar as the experiment can be programmed for their flight. Astronauts depend upon payload integration engineers to train them to conduct payload experiments. These engineers work for NASA contractors and may actually be engineers or may be aerospace technology graduates who simply receive the title of engineer from their employer. They are an important link between the contractor and NASA.

As the assigned mission nears launch, the intensity of training picks up. More flying, more simulation, direct work with mission control, and numerous simulations of the full mission will take place in final preparation for the flight. After the mission, the astronauts take part in a debriefing that lasts a few hours or a few days. This may be followed by a few days of vacation, then back to training for the next mission. If you qualify, you may be able to shoot for the stars.

Future in Space

Changes are apparent not only in aviation but also in space exploration and colonization. To some degree America has lost its fervor for space. Perhaps it has become too routine, with the Space Shuttle going into orbit nearly every month. Maybe virtual reality research, the computer age, and other concerns overshadow the spectacular accomplishments of our space program. Maybe it has become too expensive when compared to more "earthly" needs.

Lest we forget, we could fill a book with the names of practical spin-offs developed for our space program that we use daily. We should always be reminded that it was the space program that put America back on the world map of technological leadership. It was the dream of youth everywhere to become an astronaut or to be responsible for helping put astronauts into space. It was the space program that revitalized the lagging sciences within our education system. We go into space not only because we can, but also because we should.

Fortunately, a number of commercial companies are working on space programs. Other nations are investing funds, along with the United States, to keep the space program going. The Hubble Telescope is finally giving us tremendous feedback from space. We have made excellent use of satellites and should continue to deploy them. Perhaps we could reduce the number of so-called spy satellites, given the world's lessening need, and put those funds into true space research? Whatever our government decides to do, it will be because *you* took time to tell your elected representatives what *you* believe should happen with our space program. Go for it!

Major NASA Locations in the United States

NASA Headquarters
400 Maryland Avenue SW
Washington, DC 20546

Ames Research Center
NASA
Moffett Field, CA 94035

George C. Marshall Space Flight Center
NASA
Marshall Space Flight Center, AL 35812

Goddard Space Flight Center/Wallops
NASA
Greenbelt, MD 20771

John F. Kennedy Space Center
NASA
Kennedy Space Center, FL 32899

Johnson Space Center
NASA
Houston, TX 77058

Langley Research Center
NASA
Hampton, VA 23665

Lewis Research Center
NASA
21000 Brookpark Road
Cleveland, OH 44133

Stennis Space Center
NASA
SSC Station, MS 39529

10

POSTSECONDARY AVIATION PROGRAMS

YOU HAVE LEARNED that the education and technical knowledge necessary for a successful career in aerospace are available from a variety of sources. Colleges and universities represent only one type of education available. However, as aerospace becomes more technologically complex, there will be an even greater movement for colleges to solve problems and to prepare the subsequent generations for aerospace careers.

Engineers and people who work in astronautics, space sciences, astrophysics, and a variety of other physical sciences and mathematics are already prepared at the college level, many at the graduate level. Major-carrier airlines are almost exclusively hiring pilots who are college graduates. Will the national and regional airlines follow suit? The Federal Aviation Administration (FAA) is considering a much greater utilization of colleges for preparing air traffic controllers, maintenance inspectors, and electronics technicians. The way of teaching is changing. Thirty percent of U.S. postsecondary institutions already engage in distance learning, with 28 percent more making plans for such involvement. If the movement is in the direction of more education, shouldn't you consider pursuing all the education of which you are capable?

Structure of Postsecondary Aviation

More than 565 postsecondary institutions with locations in every state, as well as Puerto Rico and the District of Columbia, feature in excess of one thousand aviation-related programs. These programs range from noncredit courses of study and certificate programs to associate degree through doctorate levels. The full range of careers in aerospace is available in some form in the nation's postsecondary institutions.

Recent figures on aerospace programs indicate that there are 72 doctorate programs, 85 master's level programs, 247 bachelor's level programs, and 161 associate degree programs in our nation's colleges. The greatest number of graduate-level programs exists in two areas: aerospace engineering and astro/space physics. Table 10.1 summarizes the top five undergraduate degree areas.

Table 10.1 Collegiate Aviation Degree Programs

Program	Bachelor (No.)	Associate (No.)
Professional pilot	57	100
Management	78	50
Avionics	12	32
Maintenance	23	91
Engineering	50	9

Source: Aero-Academe

FAA Airway Science Program

The FAA sponsored a collegiate aviation program, called airway science, from 1981 through 1994. It was designed through cooperation with the University Aviation Association. The program was developed to meet the long-term needs of the FAA and the aerospace industry at large. It was offered to develop managers who have requisite expertise within an aerospace field, but who also have the skills necessary to function in today's computer-based environment. Also of top priority was the need to develop future managers with interpersonal skills that were previously missing in many technically competent persons who had risen to management levels.

Participation in the program today requires the university to submit a curriculum plan to the University Aviation Association (UAA) for approval. The UAA recognizes only five options: electronics, aviation management, professional pilot, computer science, and aircraft maintenance management. Being one of the approved institutions made the college eligible for grants from the FAA. Some grants were competitive. Some were directed to specific institutions. Nearly $60 million has been distributed to colleges since the program's inception. The FAA and the aerospace industry at large are recognizing that graduates from such approved programs are normally quality graduates who have had specific exposure desired by employers. Community college and technical institutes may partner with a four-year college or may be approved individually. Very few of the fifty-two approved institutions enjoy approval of all five options. As of this writing, there are only six colleges so approved. The FAA is withdrawing financial support from the program, but UAA will continue to approve curricula.

Internship and Cooperative Education

A host of colleges and universities are involved with the aerospace industry in providing both work experiences for students and excellent workers for the industry. Aerospace has been involved in the engineering fields for decades. Only recently has it been the practice for other areas of aerospace work to have more than token representation. If the industry truly wishes experienced persons, it must support these collegiate endeavors.

Other elements of the aerospace industry provide educational opportunities for flight dispatchers, ground service personnel, customer service agents, airport management interns, line-service workers, flight instructors, simulator instructors, and other types of related employment.

Feedback from the aerospace industry to institutions that prepare students for an aerospace career tend to mention two items of major concern. Industry prefers workers with experience and those who can communicate effectively, both verbally and in written form. This information gives you the opportunity to make a decision about getting involved in an internship or co-op program before entering college. If you do, you'll have a jump on those who do not plan ahead. Where communication is concerned, you need those skills regardless of what you choose to do. Internship and other information are available from the University Aviation Association.

Aerospace Problems to Be Solved

Aerospace is beset with major problems that must be solved if it is to continue to be the technological leader of the world. An enterprising person who can come up with practical solutions will have a great place within the industry. Some of the problems are:

- international access to airports' "open skies"
- additional airports that will handle the future hypersonic airplane and super jumbo jet
- more innovative instrument landing systems
- air safety and antiterrorism measures
- new, cleaner aviation fuels, possibly hydrogen-based, replacing fossil fuels
- more efficient helicopters and hybrid tilt-rotors
- more heliports
- support for training and educating critical personnel
- utilization of common training for military pilots and technicians
- greater environmental safeguards throughout aviation, especially near airports
- appropriate spending of aviation user fees
- government incentives for aviation entrepreneurs
- inducements for students to go into engineering and the sciences

The list could go on and on, so get involved and help solve these and other problems.

Youth Activities

Young people may gain aviation experience from a variety of sources even before they grow up. The Civil Air Patrol (a United States Air

Force auxiliary unit) has a strong volunteer youth program of more than twenty-four thousand (ages twelve to twenty-one), with many aerospace-oriented programs and curricula. It aims to enhance the leadership and life skills of cadets and to develop responsible citizens in a way similar to scouting programs. It also serves to boost interest in the U.S. Air Force and the nation. CAP annually gives out nearly $200,000 in scholarships, many flight-related.

Opportunity Skyway offers one- and two-week workshops at several locations across the nation. Skyways also has a year-round follow-up program. The Experimental Aircraft Association's Young Eagles is dedicated to flying one million youth by the turn of the century. The Boy Scouts of America offers an Exploring Division where aviation is one of the areas of exploration. And the Young Astronauts is a nationwide youth program in the United States for those who are more interested in space activities. For minority students who are interested in flying and aviation, Minority Aviation Education Association, Inc., an Indiana-based group, provides a website (maeaonline.org) with entertainment, learning tools, and scholarship information.

In Canada, the highly successful Royal Canadian Air Cadets gives 570 scholarships annually for power and glider training. There are more than twenty-eight thousand members ages twelve to eighteen in the Royal Cadets.

Several colleges offer summer programs and many state aeronautics offices sponsor summer activities. So, get involved as you are growing up and learn all you can about these fascinating careers.

Summary Comments on Aerospace Careers

Aerospace is an exciting field. It is among the most innovative of careers. It is on the frontier of new knowledge and research.

Salaries paid to workers in this industry are above the U.S. average for all career fields. The individual earning potential is among the greatest there is, when one works for someone else. The current average salary in the industry is $55,980. The majority of work is accomplished in pleasant surroundings. Benefits of working in the industry go far beyond salaries.

Workers with all kinds of talent, skills, training, and education help aerospace to be among the top U.S. industries. Quantum leaps in technology have occurred through the interaction of such workers. Greater things will come during your future work years than we might even imagine possible. However, they will not occur without effort, dedication, education and training, and a commitment to be the very best you can be.

In this author's opinion, we must reestablish the work ethic that made this nation great. A full day's work for a day's pay is required. Individual study beyond that required by teachers and schools or employers is essential. Honesty and integrity in dealing with the employer, and the employer with the contractor, is mandated. The courts, the regulators, and those who make our laws all must recommit to providing a place for the entrepreneur to thrive and to make a profit. We cannot "leave it to the other guy" to accomplish these necessary changes. It is up to each of us to get involved, to learn, to strive, and to innovate. What will you do today that will help tomorrow be better? We are not on this earth engaging in a trial run or dress rehearsal. This is our life, and we must live it to the fullest.

The shift from goods-producing to service-producing employment will continue. Service-producing industries, including transportation, will grow by 20 million jobs between now and 2010. Transportation itself is anticipated to grow to 11 million total jobs, or nearly 1.2 million new jobs in that time period. Air transportation is expected to show 20 percent total growth, with 80,000 new jobs over the next decade.

Admiral Don Engen, past administrator of the Federal Aviation Administration, once said, "Some people see a difficulty in every opportunity, while others see an opportunity in every difficulty." Which will it be for you?

Appendix A

Global and Major Airline Corporate Addresses

Airborne Express
ABX Air, Inc.
Employment Department
Airborne Air Park
145 Hunter Dr.
Wilmington, OH 45177-9390
Fax (937) 383-3838
ABX.Recruiter@airborne.com

America West Airlines
Attention: CH-EMP
4000 E. Sky Harbor Blvd.
Phoenix, AZ 85034

American Airlines
AMR Corporation
MD5651
P.O. Box 619616
Dallas/Fort Worth Airport, TX 75261-9616
(also TWA, now owned by AA)

Continental Airlines
Physical Address:
1600 Smith St.
Houston, TX 77002
Mailing Address:
P.O. Box 4607
Houston, TX 77210
Main Switchboard (713) 324-5000

FedEx Corporation
942 South Shady Grove Rd.
Memphis, TN 38120
(901) 369-3600

Northwest Airlines
Employment Center
Mailstop A1415
5101 Northwest Dr.
St. Paul, MN 55111-3034
(612) 726-2524
Job Hotline (612) 726-3600
nwajobs@nwa.com

Southwest Airlines
People Dept.
P.O. Box 36644
Mail Code: HDQ 4HR
Dallas, TX 75235

Trans World Airlines (TWA)
(see American Airlines)

United Airlines
Customer Relations-WHQPW
P.O. Box 66100
Chicago, IL 60666
(2002 note: temporary suspension of hiring activity;
do not send résumés until further notice.)

UPS Corporate Headquarters
United Parcel Service, Inc.
55 Glenlake Pkwy. NE
Atlanta, GA 30328
Employment Opportunities
(888) WORK-UPS (888-967-5877)

US Airways
2345 Crystal Dr.
Arlington, VA 22227
(703) 872-7000
Employment Opportunities
(877) USJOB4U (877-875-6248)

Appendix B

Recommended Reading

Bacon, Harold R., Michael D. Schrier, Patricia F. McGill, and Gerald D. Heilinga. *Aerospace: The Challenge.* Montgomery, AL: Civil Air Patrol, 1989. (A history of aviation/space, military, civil, and commercial flight; very readable and well illustrated.)

Bolles, Richard N. *What Color Is Your Parachute? A Practical Manual for Job-Hunters and Career-Changers.* Berkeley, CA: Ten Speed Press, 2001. (Annual guide to help one prepare for and find employment.)

Brooks-Pazmany, Deborah. *United States Women in Aviation 1919–1929.* Washington, DC: Smithsonian Institution Press, 1991. (History of aviation accomplishments by women during this time period.)

Combs, Harry, and Martin Caidin. *Kill Devil Hill.* Boston: Houghton Mifflin, 1979. (Thorough history of the genius of the Wright brothers and their invention, which changed the course of history.)

Craig, Paul A. *Be a Better Pilot: Making the Right Decisions.* Blue Ridge Summit, PA: Tab Books, 1991. (A pilot's guide to controlling human error.)

Douglas, Deborah D. *United States Women in Aviation 1940–1985.* Washington, DC: Smithsonian Institution Press, 1991. (History of aviation accomplishments by women during this time period.)

Hardesty, Von, and Dominick Pisano. *Black Wings: The American Black in Aviation.* Washington, DC: Smithsonian Institution Press, 1983. (History of aviation accomplishments of Blacks in the United States.)

Holden, Henry M. *Hovering: The History of the Whirly-Girls: International Women Helicopter Pilots.* Mt. Freedom, NJ: Black Hawk Publishing Co., 1994. (Story of women's contribution to helicopter flight.)

Oakes, Claudia M. *United States Women in Aviation 1930–1939.* Washington, DC: Smithsonian Institution Press, 1991. (History of aviation accomplishments by women during this time period.)

Schukert, Michael A. *Post-Secondary Aviation & Space Education Reference Guide.* Washington, DC: Federal Aviation Administration, 1994. (Guide to U.S. institutions offering aviation/space education programs; free from the Federal Aviation Administration.)

Wells, Alexander T. *Air Transportation: A Management Perspective.* Belmont, CA: Wadsworth Publishing Co., 1994. (A complete overview of the airline industry and its management concerns in the United States.)

ABOUT THE AUTHOR

DR. WALLACE R. MAPLES is professor emeritus of aviation and former chair of the aerospace department of Middle Tennessee State
University. Originally from Lenoir City, Tennessee, Maples's first
aviation experience was as an aviation mechanic with the United
States Army's Third Infantry Division Combat Aviation Company
at Fort Benning, Georgia. While working in that capacity, he also
took flight lessons.

After serving a tour in the army, Maples lived in southern California, where he parachuted with the Southern California Sky-
divers and worked in the early space instrumentation division of
Bourns Laboratories. He continued to take flying lessons in River-
side, California.

The need for additional education prompted Maples to return
to college. He received his bachelor's degree from Middle Tennessee State College, his master's degree from the University of
Tennessee, and his doctorate from Indiana University. He also
completed the private and commercial flight certificates.

In recent years, he has directed numerous aerospace education workshops for teachers and international seminars in fifty-seven countries, has assisted with National Aeronautic and Space Administration (NASA) seminars during several space shuttle launches, and is a past member of the board of trustees of the University Aviation Association. He also has assisted with airline training programs and served as chair of the Civil Air Patrol's National Aerospace Education Committee and president of the Tennessee Aerospace Education Association.

Dr. Maples has received awards from American Airlines: University Aviation Association's Captain W.W. Estridge, Jr. Award of Honor, 1990; United Airlines: University Aviation Association's William A. Wheatley Award, 1992; and the Frank G. Brewer Trophy in 1992, considered the most prestigious award given to an educator in the field of aerospace education. This perpetual trophy resides in the National Air and Space Museum of the Smithsonian Institution.